Also by Ladislaus Boros

WE ARE FUTURE
GOD IS WITH US
IN TIME OF TEMPTATION
LIVING IN HOPE
MEETING GOD IN MAN
THE MYSTERY OF DEATH
PAIN AND PROVIDENCE
HIDDEN GOD

MEDITATIONS

MEDITATIONS

LADISLAUS BOROS

TRANSLATED BY DAVID SMITH

DOUBLEDAY & COMPANY, INC.
GARDEN CITY, NEW YORK

Published originally under the title:
WEIHNACHTSMEDITATIONEN

Library of Congress Cataloging in Publication Data
Boros, Ladislaus, 1927–
Meditations.
Translation of Weinachtsmeditationen.
1. Jesus Christ–Nativity–Meditations. I. Title.
BT315.2.B613 1974 232.9'01
ISBN 0-385-06367-9
Library of Congress Catalog Card Number 73-22785

Printed in the United States of America

Printed in the United States of America

Contents

MEDITATIONS

Foreword

Christ, the God-man, really makes it possible to say Yes to life. He gave rest, comfort and peace from start to finish in his own life. When we meditate about his life we become Christians. Often we have an uncomfortable feeling that we have become blind to Christ; that we don't really know him any longer. But God's love for us appeared among us as a man. His word was: "Come to me and I will give you rest" (Matt. 11:28). Whenever we meet this God, it is a shattering experience because he "destroys the wisdom of the wise and thwarts the cleverness of the clever" (1 Cor. 1:19). He is a human God who can insist on our being human toward each other, with the result that he can say to us: "Come, O blessed of my Father" (Matt. 25:34). We live as Christians by thinking about his life. His own mother's life, uncomplicated, full of care, yet happy, was made completely Christian because she "kept all these things in her heart" (Luke 2:51).

The meditations in this book span a period of some ten years, but they all have certain things in common. In all of them, an attempt is made to understand the inner mystery of Christ's humanity. But above all I have tried to speak in them as Jesus spoke to us, simply and about simple things. The rich diversity of nature and all reality became clearly visible for the first time in the light of God's revelation. What couldn't be seen was proclaimed in parables.

HE DWELT AMONG US

He dwelt among us

No other Christian feast has penetrated so deeply into our experience as Christmas. Our main experience at that time is that God has said Yes to the world. He did not enter a strange world, but "came to his own home" (John 1:11). This means that our world is not just our own home—and not just our world, but our whole experience and everything that happens to us: even our very own selves. All this doesn't belong to us alone. God holds sway in everything: a dynamic quality pointing to something beyond our understanding.

What is the basic content of the birth of Jesus and how should we react to it? On the one hand, it is a message of joy. On the other, it is a call to follow Jesus. We have to bear both aspects in mind if we are to think effectively as Christians about the mystery of Christmas and really to carry out the duty it imposes on us.

A message of joy

Let us consider joy first. An angel—in other words, God himself in his mediatory form—has said to us: "I bring you good news of great joy" (Luke 2:10). There is so little joy in the world that in a sense it was necessary for an angel to come to us and call on us to live in joy. God is joy and he became man. As man, he dwelt among us. Since that time, the Christian's task has been to radiate joy into the world.

But most of the time, our life is without luster. It is narrow, colorless, and dull. We drag on our weary way, crushed by indifference. We are overworked, lonely, sick, and separated from those we love. We often find it difficult to reconcile faith with life as we experience it.

Yet the Christmas angel spoke God's word to us in that very same life: "I bring you good news of great joy!" In other words, anyone can be unhappy, but you mustn't. You have to make an effort to be happy. Put your worries aside at least today. Make this Christmas Day, the day of joy. Ask yourself something sincerely. Ask one simple question. Suppose the angel came to us today as he did to the shepherds then and said: "Be joyful." How would we answer him? Since the message of joy was given to men at the first Christmas, joy has become a duty for us as Christians and sadness is something that we ought to squash. But at once questions arise. How can we live in joy? Above all, how can we persevere in joy?

God emptied himself in Christ. He became man for us. By doing this, he showed us the way to joy. It is only in complete self-surrender that we can ever find the courage that is joy and happiness. Joy consists of complete selflessness: this can be made real only when we are face to face with our fellow men. Our neighbor does not really exist for us, however, until we serve him. We experience joy in giving joy. It is quite true to say that service of our fellow men in our everyday lives is the condition of real happiness.

There is an inescapable logic in the Christmas message: we experience joy, quite simply, in self-surrender, in giving up our lives. Joy calls for renunciation. When God became man, he became detached from himself. He gave up everything for us. Our Christian lives are also made true when we give up everything in an action that is not subject to the mood of the moment. "By this we know love, that he laid down his life for us" (1 John 3:16). We too must give up our lives for our fellow men, because our self-surrender is visible evidence of God's presence in the world and of his power over men's hearts and minds. If we feel (as we so often do) that we just can't pray any more, we should at once try to bring a little more happiness into the world. To do this is a prayer in itself, a proof that God became man.

Optimism, a "taste for happiness," is a basic and essential aspect of being a Christian. Joy is not simply a secondary accompaniment of our Christianity. On the contrary, it determines the Christian's very being. It is the note to which all the instruments at his disposal are tuned; it is the dawn heralding the day that follows. The call to experience the birth of Jesus in a really Christian way is therefore a call to banish darkness and gloom from our lives. Darkness forms no part of the Christian's experience. It is negative and bypasses the reality of Christian life: our readiness to bear witness to our joy and bring about a happy state of release and detachment in all the situations we meet with, even the most difficult.

This Christmas joy is a power that can change the world. It can give our fellow men a little more strength to carry on. Since God became man, we know that "as you did it to one of the least of these my brethren, you did it to me" (Matt. 26:31–40). Christianity is there as an event wherever our fellow men are seen in their need and are accepted by us. Whatever else we may do, however useful or even sublime it may be, is of secondary importance compared with our love of our neighbor. Christ tells us, when talking about the Last Judgment in Matthew, that the love of God is shown in our love of our neighbor. This is a fundamental and unsurpassable aspect of Jesus's birth.

The life of the child who was born for us in order to lead us from a fragmentary existence to full humanity was one of undivided faithfulness in the service of others. Christ, the God-man, gave nothing but peace until the very end of his life, his death on the cross. The angel's message was an invitation to joy, but it was more than that—it was also a duty imposed on us. A man who spent years in a labor camp in Siberia once wrote: "I looked for my God and he eluded me. I looked for my soul and I did not find it. I looked for my brother and I found all three." This summarizes perfectly the attitude that we should have toward Jesus's birth. The angel proclaimed joy: "I bring you good news of great joy." To give joy throughout the whole year would transform it into Christmas.

A call to imitation

The angel's call to joy imposed a duty on us. It was also a call to imitation. We have to realize the attitude of Christmas in our own lives, which are often so dark and gloomy. When meditating on Christ's coming, we shouldn't spend our time devising theories about the nature of being a Christian. We should try instead to draw a picture of the God who "dwelt among us": a portrait as close as possible to the reality of that God-man. What was he really like? What was man's experience of him? What power did he possess, that he could attract so many followers and inspire them with the duty of imitating him? I shall try now to describe the man in whom God's goodness lived among us.

What strikes us at once, even after the most hasty perusal of the gospels, is that *Jesus was a man of peace.* His existence had a center which was not at the mercy of the purely chance elements in life. He was also in a special sense detached from the world and from the things of the world. He had a deep equanimity, a holy indifference, transcending the deadening effect of everyday habit. He didn't bury himself in his own life or cling to himself. He wasn't enslaved by anything that was just contemporary or fashionable. He stayed open to everything new, didn't try to find confirmation of his own reality, and above all made room in his own life for everything that he encountered. He lived, as it were, away from himself, for others.

His life was in the best sense of the word *carefree.* This is clear from his own sayings. "Do not be anxious about your life." "My peace I give to you." "Do not let your hearts be troubled or afraid." "I have said this to you so that in me you may have peace." "Do not lay up for yourselves treasures on earth." "Is not life more than food and the body more than clothing?" "Which of you, by being anxious can add one cubit to his span of life?" "Seek first his kingdom, and all these things shall be yours as well." And simply: "Do not be anxious."

The man who spoke these words was never tense or fanatical. Others claimed him completely, but he was never impatient with them. He remained composed. He let himself be led forward by his fate, which he called the will of his Father, into whose hands he "commited his spirit," in other words, the center of his being. His existence was quite calm, quiet and attentive. It is true to say that he had no time for himself. The whole of his life belonged to others and, in this living for others, he was never pushing or clamorous, but utterly detached from himself.

The second quality that strikes us in God made man is that *he was closely tied to the things of this earth*. He was a man who knew what earthly things are like. He took to heart not only everything that was precious and beautiful in the world, but the ordinary, drab things of daily life. His speech was full of references to the world of nature and of man's everyday experience—"the birds in the air," "the wind and the raging waves," "the lilies of the field," the "vine," the "lost sheep," the woman leavening flour with yeast, and the thief coming by night. He spoke about kings and slaves, children and beggars, soldiers, prostitutes, tenants, priests, shepherds, and tradesmen. In his teaching and preaching he expressed the rich variety of nature and the whole of reality and human experience. What could not be seen was made visible and what could not be heard was made audible—in parables.

In his speech, Jesus tried to lead the world back to its

original simplicity. He projected the absolute into the world of things, of everyday things. The parable flowed through his speech like blood. There is a fine balance in his way of speaking—it is both directed toward the absolute and at the same time earthly. It is simple, sometimes almost obvious, very economical, natural and unaffected. Yet it betrays deep knowledge and experience and an utter certainty. It also shows how closely tied he was to the world of things. Jesus's way of speaking was that of the carpenter's son.

The third characteristic of "God's humanity" is possibly this—Jesus is to be found, not in the company of scholars and intellectuals, but *among ordinary, simple people.* This man, who was completely human because he was divinely human, looked on such people as his brothers. He didn't want to prove anything to them, and didn't want to say anything basically new to them. All he aimed to do was to reveal the shattering reality that they already knew, so that they would come to realize that they had always known it in their hearts. His only "proof" was "Truly, truly, I say to you." Knowledge and recognition are two distinct processes and Jesus made it possible for people to recognize what they had always known. There are some words which do not require proof, simply because they are spoken in so striking and original a way that they are quite translucent in themselves. In Christ, the word came into its own: it was fulfilled. When he spoke, the effect was mysterious, yet entirely simple. Words lived perfectly when he uttered them. The beatitudes, for example, could be understood by ordinary, simple people—the "babes" of Matthew's gospel—yet their meaning remained hidden from the "wise and the understanding." As a result, they were understood by only a handful of people, many of whom neither expected nor even wanted Jesus's words to be fulfilled. He therefore remained a lonely figure.

This is perhaps the most shattering aspect of Christ: that he was ***hidden***. His intention was to remain nameless. The loneliness of fulfillment was revealed in his life, the solitude that we associate with mountain heights and the depths of the ocean. Man's existence is fragmentary and fleeting. The man who, like Jesus, aims to experience the oneness of life must be prepared to remain alone. In this way, he will be able to concentrate on the unity of being. Jesus was alone as he grew up, alone in his temptation in the wilderness and alone at the most important moments of his life, in all of his most decisive actions. He moved among us like a star, suddenly and unexpectedly crossing the sky of our experience and only noticed by those who chanced to look up. His origin was unknown. He appeared, his light shone suddenly, briefly and powerfully, and he returned to the unknown. He was "a light that the darkness could not overcome" or, to use the other meaning of the Greek verb (and John was probably playing on both meanings), "light that the darkness could not understand." He was surrounded by people who didn't understand him. Laws and prohibitions, customs and traditions were quoted in argument against him and even his own mother reproached him. Everyone criticized him in one way or another, although perhaps not openly, for being different.

All the same, despite his loneliness, Jesus lived—as it were—*"easily"* on earth. He knew that his essential being would not be understood by most people, that it was inaccessible to them, but he did not worry about this, because he realized that perfect speech is usually not heard and perfect being is not perceived. He did not promise that we would *find* anything through him. He taught us, on the contrary, to *seek*, to look for the name that cannot be named. "Seek," "look for"—the notion has a central position in all that he said. It is not possible to understand his life according to the principles of our own petty selfishness. He was possessed by a holy and vital youthfulness. Nothing that was hard, inflexible or closed had any place in his life. Because his spirit was youthful and open, he was able to teach us how to be young, to be born again, to be transformed and become fresh and happy, holy in the fullest sense.

Jesus insisted that the man who did not give himself up completely could not receive the kingdom. He was our guide to a new life, the beginning of a new creation and the foundation of a new world. He called on the Christian to become a "new man," to be "born again," to renew himself every day, to look forward in hope to a "new heaven and a new earth," to sing a "new song," and altogether to be a radically transformed person. This totally new being lived in him and what he achieved was the fruit of the concentrated oneness of his being. He came "so that my own joy may be in you and your joy may be full" and "I have come so that they may have life and have it abundantly."

This "central" man was also *everybody's friend*. He reconciled and united men and made them whole. He insisted that we should not hate each other, that we should not repay evil with evil, that we should love even our enemies. Above all, he wanted to inspire everyone with hope, so that we should have the confidence to renew ourselves and live a genuine life of freedom. His rule was true and he brought everyone into his oneness without doing violence to anyone. He made it possible for us to be happy of our own accord by letting himself be disfigured by the suffering of us all. In doing this, he showed himself as a king, whose rule was true. He was united with everyone in love and mercy. "Come to me," he said, "all you who labor and are heavy laden, and I will give you rest."

He was "the light of the world," the "true light that enlightens every man." He gladly accepted publicans and sinners and told everyone that he did not condemn them. He defended sinners in the presence of so-called just men and protected children from adults. His sympathy for those he met was so great that he often wept. Men imitated him because they saw that their negligence grieved him. He was aware of the need of everyone he encountered. He perceived the need of the poor widow and gave her only son back to her. He sensed the need of the sick woman who touched the fringe of his cloak in the crowd, and cured her. He knew the need of his friend who had denied him three times and whom he looked at and forgave. His respect for every creature was unlimited, and the attention that he gave to every living being was most tender. Christ's way was the way of unlimited life lived most tenderly.

He lived a fully human life, including all the ordinary, tiring, repetitive and everyday experience of any human being. He fully accepted frustrations and temptations and, without sinning, experienced the narrow restrictions of the human condition. He was a friend of the oppressed. He also enjoyed the little things of life: a good meal, a tasty drink, a pleasant walk, a sincere friendship. When he met his fellow men, he did not dazzle them with appearances. When he suffered, he did not suffer ostentatiously, but we know that he cried out, sweated blood and felt drained and forsaken.

In this way, Christ ruled in men's lives and the kingdom of God came into being as something that could only be established by him. He threw light on the basic reality of man's existence and, as the one whose rule was true, he bore others' pain and suffering, exposing himself to all their needs. He set up his own inner truth in a world in which truth was absent, indifference prevailed, the struggle for power had captured men's hearts and confusion reigned. In this world, he had, as it were, to extinguish himself and to listen to the truth of things that was, in his case, independent of every claim to power. He had to rid himself of all illusion and keep his gaze fixed calmly, clearly, and objectively on what was essential and above all thrust aside everything in him that might prevent him from throwing light on the holiness and purity of man's being.

This attitude called for humility, renunciation, sacrifice, and a complete forgetfulness of self. The man who tries to do this has to shift the weight of his being outside himself. The whole world, unimpaired, bright and holy, is made present in a person who is really looking for the truth. Untruthfulness, on the other hand, destroys the power of man's being. It changes the world into a stage where man dissimulates in a parade of his own selfishness, an arena where every instinct to dominate is given full play. In such a world, the straight is made crooked. In a world of lies, it is no longer worth the effort to be committed to anything, to say Yes to anything with total conviction or to say No with equal determination. Freedom, humility, human togetherness, love and anger are all made impossible in such a world. What is essential becomes inessential; what is true becomes untrue; and what is human becomes inhuman. Jesus came to bear witness to the truth in that world, and the only possible end was crucifixion. Everyone who looks for truth has at some time or other been asked, in a tone of resignation, "What is truth?"

When he was crucified, Jesus forgave everyone, praying to the Father, "forgive them; for they know not what they do." He did not try to find answers to political questions or social or philosophical problems. Instead he gave hope to a broken and abandoned wretch: "Truly, I say to you—today you will be with me in paradise." It did not matter to the dying Jesus that the man had not led a decent, respectable life. He was a poor criminal who had been tied to a cross near him and could not escape death; Jesus spoke to him as the angel spoke later to Peter in prison, telling him to get up and go. But this man could not just get up and go. All the same, he obeyed and went where his nailed feet took him—to the realm of the one who is completely different. Anyone who has ever thought about a radical change in the whole of man's existence must know, after reflecting about Jesus's death, how this is accomplished: by forgiveness and by giving hope to those who seem to have no more hope.

It would be unbearable to think of Jesus having no one to help him at the end of his life, but there was someone with him who understood this complete purity and sincerity that he embodied and who could accept it entirely. That was a simple woman, his mother. Jesus found a last refuge in her, his original home. There had to be someone who was not treacherous or a coward, who did not deny the life of truth, who was not dishonest and who did not dissimulate: someone who could accept him completely.

He said very little to her from the cross. There was no need for them to say much to each other, but the few awkward words that Christ spoke to his mother and to us just before his death will live forever in men's minds. They call on us not to seek power, not to manipulate or misuse each other, not to lie and not to distort the truth. They make us conscious of our duty never to betray a friend in any way, never leave our fellow men in their loneliness, never to reject those who are abandoned, always to look for truth, and always to be aware of a person's inner attitude rather than his outward appearance. They call us, in a word, to purity. These last words which Christ spoke from the cross are utterly simple: "Behold, your mother."

This attitude, which Jesus acquired throughout his hard life, the attitude of his incarnation, became definitive in his resurrection and ascension. This was one of the essential aspects of the apostles' experience of his ascension: that goodness, forgiveness and love had become the ultimate norm. And now this attitude of Jesus's incarnation is something that cannot come to an end. God has given us Christ—a new beginning.

Christmas is more than just a mood. It is, above all, a task that we as Christians have to carry out in our lives. God became man and lived among us. He is a human God. He calls on us simply to be fully human. This humanity is lived in joy and in imitation. It is not easy to say which is more difficult to achieve nowadays. God wants us to live in joy and to imitate Jesus in our lives. This is the message of Christmas and its summons to us.

FEAST OF SILENCE

Feast of silence

When Christmas comes, many people feel a need for silence and reflection. They want to be alone for a while and to think, even though rather vaguely, about all kinds of things that have nothing to do with their everyday life. Only very few people think very deeply at this time and even fewer consciously engage in religious meditation, and when they do so, it usually takes up only a few moments of their time. It would not be wrong to say that, for almost all of us, Christmas is thoroughly profane and that what happens to us at this time is that a strange but powerful reflective mood overcomes us. But, paradoxically enough, it is often in the secular thoughts that preoccupy us at Christmas that the holy element comes close to us. This is simply because wherever we are open in our humanity the mystery of God is present among us. God is very close and can be found in the most obvious and simple things. He is closer to us than our own hearts. Having said this, we can now ask: What does the ordinary, simple person think about in those moments of silence?

What we usually experience above all then is a number of memories. Everyone of us carries with him something that is very carefully protected from the strains and stresses of everyday life. In these times of silence that occur especially at Christmas, we recall moments during which we experienced life very intensely, times of suffering, great happiness, tender love, shy friendship, or unfulfilled longing. A human face, a habitual gesture made by a long-lost friend, a color, the shape of a countryside well known in the past—these we remember, sometimes with astonishing clarity. We like to keep such memories with us, dwell on them lovingly. We feel at home in them, because what is most precious to us is made present in them. At such times we realize that our lives contain certain unique elements, experiences of special grace and power, and that even insights that we had forgotten long ago can come to light and appear totally convincing again. In those moments of recollection, too, we see with great clarity that convictions and attitudes which can barely survive the hard experience of daily life are of the greatest value and importance.

What are these convictions that are so easily broken, yet so supremely valuable? They are that it is good to be selfless, to be sad with those who mourn, to hunger and thirst for righteousness, to be pure in heart, to be merciful and to be a peacemaker. These convictions are not something that we can proclaim from the rooftops, but they are good to think about and we can savor their deep mystery when we are alone. Our everyday experience can equally well be shared and understood by others, but no one else can live out that fragile inner experience that is made present to us in those silent, lonely moments of recollection.

Whatever we may think about when we are in this mood of recollection, it will almost certainly point toward what is wonderful, mysterious, and outside the sphere of what we can perceive with our senses. This is why the birth of Jesus has always been crowned with a halo of wonder. The Christmas stories make clear what is sensed then: that man's experience, dark and confused as it is, goes much deeper than the everyday level. His longing for wonder is an authentic part of his psychology and cannot —to the regret of many theologians and philosophers—be dismissed as pure superstition. It is something that gives him the inner strength to resist the emptiness and nothingness of his existence. The truth that underlies our longing for wonder is that it is possible for us to go beyond the world of everyday experience and reach the sphere of the unsurpassable. We are not simply at the mercy of the hopeless and often bad experiences that we have in the everyday world. These do not ultimately determine what we are and what we may become. New and unexpected things can always rise up out of our lives because there is, despite all the anxiety and unhappiness that surrounds us, a hidden source of salvation in the world that can begin to flow at any time. Something that is bright and pure and not simply superstitious or wildly enthusiastic is proclaimed in this Christmas mood. It is that, despite all the evidence that exists in the world as we know it, there is a way from darkness into light: there is a light shining in the darkness of the night.

This tendency to recall the past often makes us seek the company of children at Christmas. When we are with them, we gain an insight into the mystery of childhood, but we often feel a little sad as well. What does it mean, that sadness that grips our soul when we think about our own childhood? It is above all a feeling that we have lost something quite irrevocably, the direct contact with experience that is the most striking aspect of being a child. When we were children, we could be held spellbound by things, by events and sensations, and so completely absorbed in that experience outside us that we did not glance back even fleetingly at ourselves. We were whole and undivided, and as such very close to something whole, single and undivided. At such times, it did not even occur to us to account for or justify anything. We were simply there, completely given up to that overwhelming experience with our eyes wide open.

When we recall that childhood experience, we sometimes begin to sense the real profundity of the saying which at other times seems so superficial and even sentimental—that children are angels. This does not mean that the angels are simply pretty and attractive—far from it. But angels and children are very similar in one respect—in the intensity of their being. It was precisely this that made the Austrian poet Rilke call angels "tumults of tempestuously enraptured feeling." It is not simply that they *experience* rapture in the burning transference of their whole being when they are carried away—they *are* that very rapture, that being carried away, that total self-surrender and self-forgetfulness. In this way, children are often like angels, especially when they are playing. It is also precisely this that we adults long for—our lives and sometimes even our whole appearance are usually so covered and obscured by activity, worry, self-seeking, and self-assertion.

Ordinary, simple people also give special attention to their womenfolk at Christmas, surrounding them with love and respecting above all their role as mothers, because women represent true tenderness. Tenderness is never a sign of weakness or inferiority. On the contrary, it is a readiness for love and affection which protects all that is most precious in the world and which acts with great sensitivity and restraint. Women are more directly in touch with and more deeply rooted in the mystery of life than men. They understand the confused relationships of human society more quickly and are less preoccupied with theories and concepts. They are much more concerned with life as a whole and are more intuitive.

But why is this tenderness so indispensable to life? One of the most important insights gained in recent philosophical thought is that higher, superior values often show themselves to be weak, threatened and inadequate in comparison with the lower values, those regarded as inferior. How weak human life itself was at the beginning of the evolutionary process—its origin was surrounded by accidental circumstances and it was exposed to every element of chance. How helpless man's spirit was when it began to emerge from the purely organic sphere and to achieve consciousness for the first time—seeking, hesitating and taking man further away from the warm safety of the natural basis of his life. How fragile the higher insights of man's spirits seem to be in the everyday world of today—the idea that gentleness can, for example, be stronger than violence—and how apparently unsuccessful, immature, and even antiquated or backward-looking.

How lost a quiet person can seem among fluent speakers. How vulnerable beauty is in the world of useful things. How tender hope is and how uncertain and wavering it seems when compared with the other, more obvious virtues. How little room we can make, living in a world of harsh reality, for the ethics of Jesus as outlined in the Sermon on the Mount. How quickly our dreams are shattered by the hard facts of everyday existence. How ingenuous a person seems if he tries to fulfill the demands of Christian love; if, in other words, he tries to be patient and kind, is not jealous or boastful, is not "puffed up" or rude, does not insist on having his own way, is not irritable or resentful, and puts Paul's teaching as far as he can into practice, not rejoicing at wrong, but rejoicing in the right. How strange an impression is made by the man or woman whose life is governed by such essential principles. And ultimately how impotent God seems to be in his own creation.

In this ascent of being, from the first awakening of life to its completion, one fundamental law of the universe can be perceived. The first unfolding of man's being, the upward movement of his life and his entering the ultimate reality are part of a process in which tenderness becomes more and more tender, what is threatened becomes more threatened and what is already exposed to chance becomes more exposed. The cross is in this sense the fundamental law of all life, a law which was ultimately, fully and most sublimely realized in Christ. Woman's highest vocation is to be seized by this basic law of life, to experience it, body and soul, all the time in her own life and to go out into the world thus equipped and protect it. In this way, woman shows herself to be, *par excellence*, the one who, despite all suffering, can continue to stand patiently beneath the cross waiting for a resurrection.

In addition to remembering children and our womenfolk, we also like to give special attention to old people. We want to give them happiness and be kind to them. Old people remain tied to life by very thin and easily broken threads. They are at the very end of their resources. What are the thoughts of an old person?

How quickly the years have flown by and how strange it has all been! Has my life been a dream or was it really true? So much of what I once thought important seems of little value now. My whole life seems to have flowed away from me—decisions that I have not taken, plans that I have not carried out, experiences of beauty that I have failed to appreciate, struggles in which I have taken part, perhaps in order to try to become what I have never been, at least externally. And now I am imprisoned in what I have in fact become and can never be any different. I am just this particular person and I have become what I am now, because or perhaps in spite of all the many promises in my life. Very little remains now. I have a few periods of solitude left, moments of sincere selflessness, times spent with a loved one, a few good deeds torn, as it were, forcibly from me, a certain determination to go on living, faithfulness, the persistence of hope despite all the failures of life, a helping hand, the first experience of love. Very little. What seems important to me now is what has happened as it were incidentally to me throughout my life.

These are, I think, the typical recollections of an old person who has learned the meaning of deprivation. Thinking like this, he experiences a tender love for everything that is done in vain, for what is wasted, superfluous, and foolish in the world. He feels at one with failure and imperfection, with all those who have not succeeded in life. He therefore possesses one of the rarest and most precious mysteries of all—forbearing patience. When we are caught up by the mood of Christmas, we can remember the tragic yet beautiful fate of old people and try to be very kind to them, to make up for our impatience and irritability in the past.

Children, womenfolk, and old people are not the only ones who should be in our thoughts. We should also remember with love all those who are unsuccessful, and try to give them fresh hope. The lonely too are especially in need of our presence. Refugees, prisoners, sick people, and those who have died—such people are bound to be in our minds, and their situation makes us think seriously about our own. We also think of those who are sad or unhappy, those who are full of doubt, those who no longer believe and those who cannot escape from the prison of loneliness. We should also remind ourselves of those whom we have, perhaps unintentionally, wronged, those who are hostile to us and even those people who simply do not like us. When thinking of Jesus's birth, we ought to do some good to everyone, forgive them everything and ask them to forgive us. We should be people who can offer a home to everybody.

How close to God this longing is! It is so near to the heart of our redeemer, who embraces us when we are rejected, receives the beggar, takes the one who is falling to himself and is a God of all those who stumble, who are tempted, who are outlawed and who fail. All this is very close to the God who gives his blessing to our lives, who has descended into the depths of our souls, who shook off the nocturnal shadows of death for our sake, who visits us in our loneliness and who loves the least important and the most hopeless people most tenderly of all. It is very close indeed to the God of love.

The ordinary, simple person, then, can reflect, in those few moments of silence, about all kinds of things that usually affect him at other times in only a rather superficial way. These reflections are not sublime meditations or profound thoughts. Their value, however, is to be found in the fact that they take place in a spiritual atmosphere of love and affection. They do not necessarily lead to any kind of action. All that we have to do is to dwell on them and look at life quietly, with love and without illusion. How can a person who does this be described?

He would be surprised if we were to tell him that during those quiet, reflective times he was thinking in the way that God himself thinks about us. He would never have dared to believe that God's thoughts were so simple and so obvious or that God could ever be so close to man and to all that is human. At such times, he does not ask for God at all or look for him—all that he does is to give way to the impulse of his own heart. Yet he experiences, in this mood, a God who is always near to us even if we do not seek him—"I was ready to be sought by those who did not ask for me; I was ready to be found by those who did not seek me. I said, 'Here am I, here am I.'" The same idea, expressed here by the prophet Isaiah (Isa. 65:1), was formulated by Paul in his astonishing elucidation of Deuteronomy 30:11–14 in his Letter to the Romans: "Do not say in your heart, 'Who will ascend into heaven?' (that is, to bring Jesus down) or 'Who will descend into the abyss?' (that is, to bring Jesus up from the dead). But . . . the word is near you, on your lips and in your heart" (Rom. 10:6–7).

Jesus is not a stranger to us. He is the concentration and climax of everything that is genuine and true in our existence, of all self-surrender and of all the help we give to others. In his quiet thoughts, the ordinary, simple person senses Jesus's presence as his eternal brother and in his heart as the center of his human activity, even if he does not consciously think of, or feels that he is a long way from Jesus.

LOVE

Love

It would be unthinkable if I did not include among these meditations some thoughts about the fundamental Christian attitude of love. The word "love" has, of course, become notoriously ambiguous in recent years and it may always have been so. But, despite all the high-flown things that have ever been said about it, the only people who really understand love in its essence are those who have personally experienced it. The Christian answer, then, to the question: "What is someone leading an authentic, radical human life really like?" is simply—such a person is one who loves.

We must try to express in words at least some fragment of this human longing for love which all of us experience at some time or other in our lives. Perhaps—who knows—we may succeed in painting an authentic picture which is very close to the reality that we call love, that presence which we sense within us and which we almost take for granted, however mysterious and almost incomprehensible it may be. Love rises up, an inner necessity, almost a compulsion, from the depths of our unconscious and, as soon as we become aware of it, takes control of us completely. When we once begin to love, we can do nothing else but love. Love is a strange urge within us, so strong that it sometimes hurts us and at others can even have a catastrophic effect on our lives and those of others. It is therefore very important that we should learn how to love, how to take in hand this powerful impulse that rises up so mysteriously within us and overwhelms the whole of our being. We cannot allow it to run riot, give it free rein to go where it will, without any aim or sense of direction. We have to fashion and direct it, let it fulfill itself or even prevent it from being fulfilled. Formed and controlled in this way, love becomes a mature, authentic virtue, in other words, a practiced and painfully disciplined attitude toward the world. If love is not really learned, it may result in unmeasurable pain and suffering. This is the paradox of love—that we are bound to love and that we must at the same time learn to love through pain and adversity. Simply to let love remain at the stage of pure, uncontrolled feeling is to let it enflame us with demonic and even destructive power.

It is advisable, then, to be very cautious of using high-flown language in speaking of love. Tender things must be handled tenderly. We should therefore approach this sublime reality of human life as something holy and of great value and, before we enter its mystery, open the door of our mind very gently and tune our thoughts delicately into it. In the history of Western spirituality, no text contains such essential truths about love as a practiced Christian attitude as Chapter 13 of Paul's first Letter to the Corinthians. So important is this text that we cannot do better than to meditate about it here and to allow its message to enter our hearts. It is possibly the most concentrated and meaningful expression in the world of all that is essential in the Christian attitude!

"If I speak in the tongues of men and of angels, but have not love, I am a noisy gong or a clanging cymbal. And if I have prophetic powers, and understand all mysteries and all knowledge, and if I have all faith, so as to remove mountains, but have not love, I am nothing. If I give away all I have, and if I deliver my body to be burned, but have not love, I gain nothing.

"Love is patient and kind; love is not jealous or boastful; it is not arrogant or rude. Love does not insist on its own way; it is not irritable or resentful; it does not rejoice at wrong, but rejoices in the right. Love bears all things, believes all things, hopes all things, endures all things.

"Love never ends; as for prophecies, they will pass away; as for tongues, they will cease; as for knowledge, it will pass away. For our knowledge is imperfect and our prophecy is imperfect; but when the perfect comes, the imperfect will pass away. When I was a child, I spoke like a child, I thought like a child, I reasoned like a child; when I became a man, I gave up childish ways. For now we see in a mirror dimly, but then face to face. Now I know in part, then I shall understand fully, even as I have been understood. So faith, hope, love abide, these three; but the greatest of these is love" (1 Cor. 13:1–13).

This text is an astonishing mixture or succession of statements, demarcations, contrasts, and interpretations. We shall consider it above all with what it has to say about man and his attitudes and thought in mind, in other words, from the anthropological and philosophical points of view, and we shall see, as we examine the text more closely, that it is impossible to speak effectively about love in any other way. What is most remarkable is that Paul makes no attempt to define love as such. There is a demarcation—in other words, he marks love off from other gifts and virtues—but no definition. He also enumerates the qualities of love and circles around them. This process reveals a very important aspect of love—that it has above all to be experienced. We have to be shattered by it. Love is a primordial experience in our lives. Its essential, original, and fundamental aspect, however, always eludes our grasp and we can therefore never discuss it. The essence of love is simply given to us as an experience. This experience is first of all that:

Love is everything.

If I speak in the tongues of men and of angels, but have not love, I a noisy gong or a clanging cymbal.

We do not need to examine in detail here what Paul was saying to the Christians at Corinth—we should rather try to discover what his own experience was. It is clear that there were people in the community there with special spiritual gifts who had reached the ultimate point of human experience and were able to express (in hesitant, stammering language, it is true) the inexpressible. The historical and psychological details of this "speaking in tongues" are of secondary importance to us here. What is above all important, however, is the fundamental experience that, however beautifully you may speak, as beautifully as any man or even with the eloquence of an angel, if you lack love it is just "sounding brass," empty nonsense, and you have neither done nor even experienced what really matters. Your speaking sounds good, it may even move your listeners, but what lies behind it? Nothing. Emptiness. You utter words, but the reality is not contained in them. What you say, your talk, your sermon, your lecture, may be stimulating, inspiring, very touching and excellent in many ways, but you yourself are not behind it and so it lacks meaning and content and ultimately leaves people sad. You are only looking for yourself and trying to make an impression.

For Paul, love is first and foremost service of others: action. If you have never loved, how can you dare to speak about the reality of love? You will simply be presenting a favorable picture of yourself in words that will quickly be lost. First prove that you value the other person more than your own life and that you will defend him from the cares of the world and the injuries it can inflict. Give him shelter. Protect him, if necessary against himself. Fight for him, give him life, let him grow and expand inwardly. Talking about love is, for Paul, empty and hollow without the experience and action of love. We have first to prove in our lives that our words are sincere. It is very easy to deceive other people. Even very substantial talking is of no use at all if love is absent from it. Love communicates itself in silence, by simply being and remaining there, giving help and support. Anyone can utter fine words—it depends on his sensitivity to language and his gift for speaking. The true language of love, however, sounds quite different. What is heard in it is not emotion or even intelligent reasoning, but self-surrender.

And if I have prophetic powers, and understand all mysteries and all knowledge, and I have faith, so as to remove mountains, but have not love, I am nothing.

Another, even more striking demarcation. A prophet is a person who can interpret the events of this world in the light of God's grace. A man can "understand mysteries" when he is able to remain in the presence of the inexplicable and grasp it with the whole strength of his being, penetrating ever more profoundly into the hidden truth at its center. A man "has faith" when, perhaps despite inner doubts, he exposes himself to a reality which cannot be constructed from the material of this world. He has faith when he allows himself to be claimed in the depths of his being by the absolute which he cannot explain. He has faith when the inner power that comes from his being claimed in this way enables him from time to time to do things which amaze the world and which can, in other words, "move mountains." These three qualities, prophecy, knowledge, and faith, together provide a very impressive picture of the deep reality of human life, that of prophetic, knowing, and believing existence. In the anthropological sense, it is a picture of man's fundamental and all-embracing dynamism, his essential reality. Yet even to this, Paul says, prophecy, knowledge, and faith are very important, beautiful, and indeed indispensable, but they are not the most essential or the ultimate human reality. That reality is love.

When, then, is that love to which Paul gives such priority? The more firmly he marks love off from the other spiritual gifts, the more distinctly it can be seen that if we have not love, we are nothing.

If I give away all I have, and if I deliver my body to be burned, but have not love, I gain nothing.

Karl Barth said: "There is a love which is without love, a self-surrender which is not surrender, a paroxysm of self-love which has the external appearance of an authentic love of God and our brother, the love which will go to the ultimate limits of self-surrender, but which is in reality not at all concerned with God and our brother . . . Only love itself counts; no acts of love as such, not even the greatest. These can also be done without love and they are then meaningless. Even worse—they are often done against God and our brother."

Love has previously been described as action, but here selflessness is added as an essential element of love. Although it is also possible to look for oneself in "love," it is equally possible to lose that love in unselfish activity. There is a strange and little recognized quality of love which can best be described as not knowing about oneself, not regarding oneself, or as an absence of intention. A man can give up everything, he can even go so far as to lay down his life, but if this is not done quite gratuituously it is nothing.

This brings us to the ultimate limit of what can be expressed by language. We can perhaps say that love is simply as the psalmist said: "I have become a beast of burden before thy face." This not knowing about oneself, this pure self-surrender, this wanting nothing from the other person, this acceptance of being a stranger—all this is love. Without this fundamental selflessness, we are nothing, however many acts of love we may perform. If we are not totally selfless, we do not really love—all that we are doing is looking for ourselves. Anyone who has ever loved knows that it is possible to put another person in the wrong even by being good to him, to do him an injury by giving oneself completely to him. If we remain attached to ourselves while loving, it is not love at all.

The underlying thought of this astonishing text is inexorable, but it is ultimately consoling, because it reveals to us the real dimensions of our own humanity. Strangely enough, however, Paul's teaching about love now abruptly follows a different and unexpected direction. He describes, first positively and then negatively, the qualities of this essential human attitude of love, although he had previously hinted that he could not speak about it at all.

The qualities of love

Paul's description of love is, of course, very fragmentary. One has the impression that he has himself experienced love in its essence and that he cannot speak about it precisely for this reason. His ideas in this passage come not so much from his intellect as from his heart, so that they have a strange logic that can only be understood by the heart. This deep experience of love enables him to release, as it were, fragments of intuitive knowledge, each one of which goes to the heart of the matter.

Love is patient. This description of love begins with an apparently insignificant but in fact living quality—patience. It is this quality that makes it possible for a person to persevere with someone else for a long time, even until death: for him to bear with that other person, not in indifference and neglect, but in creative faithfulness. Patience is the courage to bear with others, to help them to bear their own existence. It is the courage to go on in time and to give oneself to others perhaps in new and different ways. It is the courage not to cut through the thread of love and to show, by our presence, that the other person can rely on us in all the different situations of life, that we will remain with him. Without this courage to give ourselves faithfully and patiently for a long time, the proximity of other people can be a form of hell.

The Christian whose aim is to love authentically and thus to become fully and authentically a human being has to educate himself to be faithful to the point of being ready to give up everything. He must never capitulate, but persist to the end. His life's task is to overcome disagreements, however long this may take, and patiently to learn how to control the fluctuating impulse of love. Seen in this way, love can find its true expression in our being unconditionally present for other people forever.

Love is kind; love is not jealous or boastful. This quiet, humble and long-suffering patience, which reveals itself as a complete openness to others in all the situations of life, has to be accompanied by kindness, a friendliness, a peaceful serenity in being together with others—a togetherness that is always threatened by nervous agitation and a loss of peace—a silent acceptance of others' failings, their fickleness, their inner restlessness and their physical and spiritual imperfections and a tender, considerate, and sympathetic forbearance. A love that is kind will moreover not be jealous. In other words, the person who loves patiently and kindly will not seek recognition. He will not set himself against other people, try to put them in the wrong or list their faults and failures. He will not allow himself to be affected by a bitter and unhealthy animosity toward his fellow men which would eventually undermine his whole existence and which is ultimately only a form of self-righteousness.

The person who loves kindly and not jealously will also, Paul insists, not be boastful. This means, surely, that he will not thrust himself forward, seeking admiration on the one hand or pity on the other. On the contrary, he will be ever ready to listen to others.

How clear, simple, and translucent the love of which Paul speaks is! Yet how much effort it calls for every hour and every day of our lives if we are to overcome ourselves and achieve it! It is often the most insignificant and obvious things which help us to acquire the most profound attitude toward ourselves and others. But, in our attempt to make these obvious things (which we take so much for granted) realities in our daily lives we often begin to perceive that they are not so obvious and that they cannot simply be accepted without question.

Love is not arrogant or rude. Love does not insist on its own way. Paul now approaches his task from another direction, using as it were the concave mirror of negation to reveal the shape of love. We should note the order in which he lists these negative attributes of love. The first is that love is not arrogant or, more literally, not inflated—"not puffed up" in the older translation. This points to a very important quality of love which is at once visible—especially in the image that Paul uses—but which can be expressed in words only with difficulty.

The man who truly loves does not make himself bigger than he really is. He does not fill himself with emptiness. He does not regard himself, his intentions or his aspirations as too important, does not give them an exaggerated value. He does not fill the entire sphere of human existence with himself—on the contrary, he prefers to withdraw to the periphery to allow life to move freely and to thrive. He does not fill himself with meaningless, unimportant things, but leaves room for the other person's life to flow into his own, opens himself to the other's vitality, happiness, ideas, and feelings. The loving man fills himself from the other person. It is indeed only the man who can receive the gift of his neighbor's being who really loves. Being "puffed up" is denying all room to the other person and placing exclusive emphasis on oneself. Love, on the other hand, means restraint, inner detachment, never stressing oneself. Love underemphasizes itself, takes little account of itself, gives to others what it probably denies itself and is even glad that others are greater. Such love is a pure love.

This pure quality of love can be seen in that love is "not rude." Paul is not moralizing here—he is pointing rather to an inner process, the sensitivity of the person who loves. It is not possible to love rudely or oafishly because one is so completely seized by the other person's whole being that one has to be polite toward him. This courteous attitude arises, as it were, from an inner impulse. Its opposite, the brutalization of love, is expressed in the disappearance of polite behavior. There is an element of nobleness in love—it acknowledges the other person's essential goodness and makes him feel that he is valued. It tones down our natural violence and ensures that nothing disastrous or painful will occur in our relationships. This polite aspect of love means, above all, that life is made possible for other people, that unpleasant situations will be smoothed over, that other people's vulnerability will be borne in mind and that their dignity will be respected.

This results in the essential definition of love, that it does not insist on its own way. This is, however, infinitely difficult. At some time or another, each one of us experiences a certain disgust—it is so humiliating to be the person we are, always the same, always leading the same miserable existence. We all want to get on in the world, even at somebody else's expense. We believe that we are disappointed by everyone and can escape from ourselves. There is in this a danger which threatens the very essence of love, namely the temptation to use other people to give strength and support to ourselves. How can we overcome the urge to do this?

Once again, we are brought to the ultimate limit of what can be expressed in words. The only possible answer to this question is, I think, that we can overcome this impulse only by loving. The great mystery of love is that it is a detachment from oneself which defies further investigation and which can "playfully overcome," as Karl Barth observed, the dark temptation which "tries to overcome love in people who love." By loving, love cannot simply seek itself—it is incapable of doing this.

Paul's thought now takes a fresh turning once more and he describes the victory of love in everyday life.

Love is not irritable or resentful; it does not rejoice at wrong, but rejoices in the right.

An essential aspect of love is that in it we are released from a negative attitude. Our fellow men do not get on our nerves, annoy us or drive us into an attitude of hostility toward them. On the contrary, love completely overcomes all irritability and animosity. It does this, above all, by not being resentful; in other words, by not listing the other person's failings or, to translate Paul's text more literally, by not making an account of his evil. The man who loves authentically is simply unable to pronounce that completely perverse saying, unfortunately so often heard: "I can forgive, but I cannot forget." Reckoning, making an account of evil, can in time result in the person whom we love most of all becoming a monster, something that we can no longer bear to see or be with. So one of the most essential qualities of love is that it does not reckon or make entries in the accounts.

The "released" attitude of love, moreover, has nothing to do with the mentality that "rejoices at wrong" or with the meanness of spirit that derives satisfaction from another person's mistakes or from the thought that he has at last made a complete fool of himself. Love is absent from the life of a person who rejoices at wrong in this way. It is only a step from this to pride, to daring to say to the God who was crucified and rejected for us: "Lord, I thank thee that I am not like other men, extortioners, unjust, adulterers, or even like this tax collector" (Luke 18:11). The man who loves, on the other hand, is, according to Paul, a man who "rejoices in the right." This love is a deep joy in the element of light in the other person's existence. A profound benevolence. I rejoice that the other person has reached a higher level of consciousness, or freedom, perhaps even of success, of selflessness and of self-surrender. This is the attitude with which God has confronted us since the creation of the world and will continue to confront us in eternity and which John defined in very simple words, but words which express the very essence of Christian faith: "God is greater than our hearts" (1 John

3:20). To be able to rejoice sincerely in the other person's fine and admirable characteristics is one of the greatest of all acts of selfless love.

Mature love

The demands that have been made in the verses that we have considered so far are so overwhelming that Paul seems at this point to become suddenly aware of the fact that the level of love in the form in which he has outlined it simply cannot be reached by man. We have therefore to be patient with ourselves. If we really want to learn how to love, we must again and again make a new beginning, at the same time persisting in what we can still continue to do despite repeated failures. We must, in other words, allow our love gradually to become mature. Paul suggests four points of departure in this process of growth.

Love bears all things, believes all things, hopes all things, endures all things. He first introduces four simple concepts—bearing, believing, hoping, and enduring. How often we are exploited when we love! We are so vulnerable in love, losing ourselves and being treated as playthings. How often the other person seems to make light of our love. The disappointment that results when the other does not respond to our love has to be borne, endured in faith and hope. How often we feel tired of loving and long to give it up. We find it impossible to bear the failure of trying to go on loving, we cannot believe the other person any more because we feel that we are being deceived—and may even have proof of it. We can no longer hope for any radical change. Such a love cannot, we think, possibly endure.

If we are honest, however, we must try to look at the matter from the other side. There are clearly situations in which what we believed was love has never become a real state of togetherness, and in such cases we should go no further. On the other hand, if we have already entered into what may be a painful relationship, we should then bear, believe, hope and endure. What would become of our world if no one were to persist in loving?

These four qualities of mature love fundamentally express one single attitude—that I make it possible, by my selfless love, for the other person to love as well, for him to feel, when I am with him, that he is quite secure with me, that he can be himself, the person he is or would like to be, that I do not restrict him, do not reproach him for being what he is, do not see him simply as he ought to be. It may be that new possibilities will be brought to life within him, not at once, of course, but gradually, as love continues to flow into him. I may succeed in this way in awakening him to his real humanity.

Love never ends; as for prophecies, they will pass away; as for tongues, they will cease; as for knowledge, it will pass away. Here Paul returns to his first idea, but does so, as it were, by way of a spiral staircase ascending to a higher level. At the end of our life, we shall not possess our achievements or our gifts—our real and eternal life is built up simply and solely of this bearing the burden of love. Everything that we have ever known, everything that has so profoundly shaken us throughout our life, everything that we have ever done to control the world, all our achievements—all this will pass away in a radical transformation. Only love is radically unchangeable. Only love will accompany us intact when we enter the area of eternal fulfillment. Love is the presence of the promise already fulfilled. This thought is expressed in Paul's statement about perfection and imperfection, in which our successes are given a relative value:

For our knowledge is imperfect and our prophecy is imperfect; but when the perfect comes, the imperfect will pass away. We can never really complete or fulfill anything in life. Our desires, longings and aims reach out into the future, but their realization always lags behind. Only love lasts. Everything else can only be carried out imperfectly, in part. What may have seemed to us years or even only months ago to be quite obvious, something that we took completely for granted, is suddenly seen to be wretched and meaningless, perhaps not entirely valueless, but certainly imperfect.

When this happens, we become aware of a deeper level of experience, of a longing for quiet recollection, of a need to pause and reflect. We have, however, to learn what to do during this silence; otherwise, something will wither away in us and we shall remain at the mercy of fragmentary thoughts, and restless desires and fears. We have to learn how to dwell on one really serious question or one really important thought. It is only when we have made this practice of silence a way of life that we shall begin to have a true inward experience and that something will emerge from our existence—wisdom, quiet understanding, or simply love.

Love remains. Only love can make life truly one, reconcile differences, overcome divisions, achieve a harmony between the contrasts and contradictions that make our thinking and speaking so difficult or make us at one with our friends, with nature and with ourselves. Without love, we ourselves remain imperfect, strangers in a strange world. This is why Paul goes on to say: *When I was a child, I spoke like a child, I thought like a child, I reasoned like a child; when I became a man, I gave up childish ways.*

Paul is not speaking against the childlike quality that is praised so highly in the gospels: that simplicity and directness of heart so characteristic of children. He is not opposed to that inherent ability to perceive and to be fully conscious without any ulterior intention that children possess. All of these are distinctively human qualities which are both noble and very difficult for an adult to acquire. Paul is referring here to the childish characteristic in man which prevents him from becoming mature and which makes him cling to what is passing. We say that a child is *childlike,* but that an adult who goes through life as if it were a game, without accepting his responsibilities, is *childish.* This irresponsible and childish way of thinking, speaking, acting, and judging prevents a man from loving.

Love, after all, brings with it a special kind of seriousness, even a threatening need. In love, we have to persist. We cannot play with love or act irresponsibly with it. It is by exposing ourselves to the care, the gravity and the fatigue of love that we grow toward what is essential in life and become mature. It is only in that way and in the degree to which we grow toward love that "birth" will take place in our lives. But toward what future is this human birth which takes place in love directed?

The future of love

What precisely is the promise of life that has become mature in love? Paul expresses this promise in three sentences.

The first is *For now we see in a mirror dimly, but then face to face.* Our seeing now, Paul says, is fragmentary, partial, always reversed, as in a mirror, and always, because the mirror that he had in mind was of polished metal, very indistinct, a reflection with vague outlines. Our experience of the ultimate reality of God is in concepts and notions. It is not an experience of direct personal encounter with him. Our experience of almost everything is reversed—God is very close to us, yet we think of him as far away; he is far from us, but we think that he is near.

Then, however (that is, when we really love), Paul continues, this way of seeing and experiencing will be totally transformed. God will become a person whom we shall see "face to face." We shall see each other directly, without any intermediary. We shall be personally in touch with each other. According to the degree to which I love, something will happen between God and me, the experience which friends and lovers glimpse fleetingly in moments of supreme awareness—that I am you and you are me. Love can, Paul suggests, be fulfilled absolutely.

Now I know in part, then I shall understand fully, even as I have been understood. This apparently insignificant second sentence contains the whole promise of our life on earth. We shall know God as he knows us. In other words, we shall enter his immediate presence and see him directly. We shall still be creatures, but we shall understand God with every fiber of our being as he understands us. Basically, this means that we shall become God. The fundamental dynamism of my existence on earth is a movement, a growth into the absolute.

So faith, hope and love abide, these three; but the greatest of these is love. Even in this eternal confrontation, faith and hope remain in a very real sense, even though they will be transformed into a direct relationship with God. Faith remains as a constant state of being face to face with each other and a loving desire to receive. Hope remains as an ability and a will to receive even more of the eternal love. But these two must change their earthly forms. They will not exist then in the obscure and ever shifting forms that they have here on earth—they will remain as a bright, radiant, and happy growing into a similarly ever-growing God.

In the second century A.D., Irenaeus of Lyons commented on this passage in Paul: "God must always be the greater, not only in this world, but also in eternity. He is always the one who teaches and man is always the one who learns. As the Apostle has said, when everything else has passed away, these three will remain—faith, hope, and love. Our faith in God our teacher remains unshakable and we hope to receive even more from him . . . because he is goodness and because he possesses inexhaustible wealth and a kingdom without end."

But why is love the greatest of these? It is because only love can be fulfilled without changing its present form. Our faith and hope are at present fragmentary. They remain in eternity, but have to be given an essentially new form, that of a certain, peaceful movement or growth into God which is also eternal because God is infinite. Only love, however, remains then as it is now—if and insofar as it is really love. This means that love can and must, even now, be interpreted as the ultimate anticipation of the ultimate. It is the presence of heaven in our life here on earth, the presence of the ultimate in our imperfect existence here and now. Love is also the mystery of Jesus's birth.

PROMISE

Promise

We cannot do better, when meditating on the mystery of Jesus's birth, than to think about another mystery—that of a young woman who called herself "Sister Teresa of the Child Jesus." Perhaps she can tell us more than the earnest and important men of whom we hear so much.

Teresa of Lisieux was only twenty-four when she died. A great deal has been written about her and many people have prayed to her and thought about her "Little Way" of holiness. Although there is much piety in her writings, there is also much that is contradictory. Her language was florid, but her style, like her way of life, was also often bold and daring. She lived with reckless abandon.

What has Saint Teresa to say to us that is relative to our meditation? If we are to understand the mission of this quite extraordinary girl, we must look into her autobiographical writings. These are now available in their original form.* Like most unusual people, Teresa thought in

* St. Thérèse of Lisieux, *Autobiography of a Saint,* The complete and authorized text of *L'Histoire d'une âme,* translated by Ronald Knox, with a Foreword by Vernon Johnson (New York: P. J. Kenedy & Sons, 1958: the page numbers of quotations and citations in this meditation refer to this edition); *Therese vom Kinde Jesus. Selbstbiographische Schriften* (Einsiedeln, 1958); André Combes, *Sainte Thérèse de Lisieux et sa mission* (Paris, 1955); *Thérèse von Lisieux, Geschichte einer Seele und weitere Selbstzeugnisse,* collected, translated and introduced by Otto Karrer (Lugano, 1947).

images. This is an extremely subtle way of combining the tension within the soul with the earthly element, and of expressing the mysteries inherent in the writer's concrete existence. If we wish to understand the mystery of Teresa's life, we must first look carefully at the images in which she saw her life's task reflected. What, then, were the images that figured most prominently in her spiritual life? The first that comes to mind is clearly connected with the mood of Christmas.

The stars: "Sunday passed too quickly . . . not without a hint of melancholy. Up to the time of Compline, I remember, my happiness was unalloyed; it was during Compline that I said to myself: 'The day of rest will soon be coming to an end.' Tomorrow I should have to pick up life again, do my work and learn my lessons—it gave me the sense of being an exile, longing for the eternal rest of heaven, those endless sabbaths . . . On the way home I would look up at the stars that shone so quietly and the sight took me out of myself. In particular there was a string of golden beads (Orion's belt) which seemed, to my great delight, to be in the form of the letter T. I used to show it to Papa and tell him that my name was written in heaven" (pp. 66–67). We should not forget, when we read this, that Teresa's "memories" were not simply memories, but interpretations of God's presence in her life.

The child: Teresa always thought of herself as a child. In answer to the question: "What would you do if you could begin your religious life all over again from the beginning?" she replied: "I think I would do the same again . . . I could never fear damnation. Little children are not damned. They are judged with special leniency. It is possible too to remain a child even in the most responsible tasks. Is it not said of them that the Lord will be exalted in order to comfort all the gentle and lowly on earth?"

She also maintained that perfection had always seemed to her to be something quite simple. "It is sufficient to recognize that one is nothing and to place oneself like a child in the arms of God. All the fine books that I cannot understand, let alone put into practice, I leave to greater souls and exalted spirits. I am glad that I am little, because the heavenly banquet is reserved for children and for those who are like them."

"For some time past," Teresa wrote, "I have indulged the fancy of offering myself up to the Child Jesus as a plaything, for him to do what he liked with me. I don't mean an expensive plaything; give a child an expensive toy, and he will sit looking at it without daring to touch it.

"But a toy of no value—a ball, say—is all at his disposal: he can throw it on the ground, kick it about, make a hole in it, leave it lying in a corner, or press it to his heart if he feels that way about it. In the same way, I wanted Jesus to do exactly what he liked with me . . . and he'd taken me at my word" (p. 171).

All this shows us how mature this attitude of being a child in God's presence is. There is nothing sentimental about it. Above all, we are aware of the positive value of Teresa's conviction that we should place ourselves entirely at the mercy of the whims of a child and that, because that child is God-man, we shall, by doing this, come closer to God.

The sea: "I was seven or eight years old when Papa took us to Trouville, and I shall never forget the impression made on me by my first sight of the sea. I couldn't take my eyes off it, its vastness, the ceaseless roaring of the waves, spoke to me of the greatness and the power of God . . . That evening, about the time when the sun looks as if it were sinking into an endless waste of waves, and leaving a long track of light in between, Pauline and I were sitting on a rock by ourselves watching it . . . For a long time I sat there thinking about this track of light and of its heavenly counterpart—the grace which pierces the darkness and guides the little white-sailed ship on its course. Sitting there beside Pauline, I made a resolve that I would always think of our Lord as watching me" (pp. 74–75).

This is another indication of how directly God flowed into the soul of this child through his creation. She consciously chose to find God in all things.

The Little Flower: "If a wild flower could talk, I imagine it would tell us quite candidly about all God has done for it; there would be no point in hushing up his gifts to it, out of mock humility, and pretending that it was ugly . . . Anyhow, this isn't going to be the autobiography of a flower like that. On the contrary, I'm delighted to be able to put them on record, the favors our Lord has shown me, all quite undeserved" (p. 36).

Let us try to understand this "florid" but honest language. Teresa thought of herself as a flower, a little wild flower. She grew out of the earth and flowered without any merit on her part or any effort. She was simply a gift of grace.

The basket: "A day came when Léonie, thinking she was too old now to play with dolls, came along to us with a basket full of dresses and pretty little bits of stuff for making others, with her own doll lying on the top. 'Here you are, darlings,' she said, 'choose which of these you'd like; they're all for you.' Céline put her hand in and brought out a little ball of silken braid which had taken her fancy. I thought for a moment, and then said, as I held out my hand: 'I choose the whole lot!' Then, without further ceremony, I took over the whole basket . . . Only a childish trait, perhaps, but in a sense it's been the key to my whole life" (p. 51).

Later, Teresa wrote: "Forgive me, Jesus, if I overstep the bounds of right reason in telling you about these longings and hopes of mine, which overstep all bounds; and heal the hurt of my soul by granting all these wishes fulfillment. To be betrothed to you, to be a Carmelite . . . surely that ought to be enough for anybody? But, somehow, not for me . . . I feel as if I were called to be a fighter, a priest, an apostle, a doctor, a martyr; as if I could never satisfy the needs of my nature without performing, for your sake, every kind of heroic action at once.

"I feel as if I'd got the courage to be a Crusader . . . dying on the battlefield in defense of the Church. And at the same time, I want to be a priest; how lovingly I'd carry you in my hands when you came down from heaven at my call . . . Insignificant as I am, I long to enlighten men's minds as the prophets and doctors did; I feel the call of an Apostle. I should like to travel all over the world, making your name known and planting your cross on heathen soil; only I shouldn't be content with one particular mission, I should want to be preaching the gospel on all five continents and in the most distant islands, all at once. And even then it wouldn't do, carrying on my mission for a limited number of years; I should want to have been a missionary till the world came to an end . . . What are you going to say to all these fond imaginations of mine? . . . Why, in consideration of my weakness, you found a way to fulfill my childhood's ambitions, and you've found a way now to fulfill these other ambitions of mine, world-wide in their compass" (pp. 233–34).

How wonderfully consistent Teresa's spiritual life was. Both as a little girl and later as a nun, she wanted to have everything—first the basket and then absolutely everything. And in the end she received everything.

Nature: "Our eyes were lost in distance, as we watched the pale moon rising slowly above the height of the trees. Those silvery rays she cast on a sleeping world, the stars shining brightly in the blue vault above us, the fleecy clouds floating by in the evening wind—how everything conspired to turn our thoughts toward heaven! How beautiful it must be if this, the obverse side of it, was so calm and clear!" (p. 134). In another part of her autobiography, Teresa says: "At all the critical moments of my life, I've found that nature seems to be the mirror of my own soul's condition: heaven shed tears in sympathy with me, and a cloudless sun shone brightly on my days of happiness" (p. 142).

Teresa's description of her experience in Switzerland, when she was on her way to Rome with the intention of asking Pope Leo XIII for his permission to enter the convent at the age of fifteen, is very interesting.

Switzerland: "Rome was our goal, but there were plenty of wonderful experiences on the way there. Switzerland, where the mountain tops are lost in cloud, with its graceful pattern of waterfalls, its deep valleys where the ferns grow so high and the heather shows so red! How deeply it affected me, this lavish display of natural beauty! That God should have seen fit to squander such masterpieces on a world of exile . . . ! I was all eyes as I stood there, breathless at the carriage door; I wished I could have been on both sides of the compartment at once, so different was the scenery when you turned to look in the other direction. Now we were on the mountain side, with a bottomless chasm beneath ready to engulf us; now we would pass some delightful village, its chalets and its church tower covered with a soft canopy of snow-white cloud, or a wide lake at evening, with its calm surface reflecting at once the blue sky and the glow of sunset, till it has all the beauty of fairyland. Far away on the horizon we could see the great mountains, shadowy in outline except where their snow-clad tops showed dazzling in the sun, to complete the splendor of the view. The sight of these beauties made a deep impression on my thoughts. I felt as if I were already beginning to understand the greatness of God and the wonders of heaven" (pp. 157–58).

Do I have to add anything to this? Nothing, except gratitude that God has given us a country which, in 1887, inspired the soul of this holy young woman with such thoughts.

Wax and the canary: "A relation of our nurse died quite young, leaving a family of three babies; and during her illness we took in the two little girls . . . Seeing these innocent souls at close quarters, I realized what a mistake it is not to train them from the very start, when they are like wax to receive impressions . . . I saw what Jesus meant about hurting the conscience of 'one of these little ones'" (p. 146). This thought is at once taken to a deeper level in Teresa's description of another experience a little later—that of her pet birds.

"I had a canary once that sang to perfection; and at the same time I had a linnet which I tended with great care because I'd taken charge of it before it could fly. Born to captivity, it had no parents to learn from; but when it heard the canary trilling all day, it tried to follow suit. Not easy for a linnet; his gentle voice wasn't up to the shrill notes of his music master. It was touching to witness his efforts, but they succeeded in the end; without losing the sweetness of his voice, he sang in canary fashion" (p. 147).

Two impressive images of the spiritual life—the wax taught Teresa that man is fashioned by God and receives, as it were, his fingerprints and the linnet showed her that he can learn quite different "tunes" from those that are inborn.

Penance: Before she entered the convent at Lisieux, Teresa prepared herself carefully, but perhaps rather strangely, for the great day.

"How did I pass those three months, a time, as it proved, so full of graces? My first thought was that perhaps I'd better give up living by a rather strict rule, as my habit had been of late . . . But before long I came to realize that this respite was a precious opportunity, and decided to give myself up, more than ever, to a recollected and mortified way of life. When I say 'mortified,' I don't mean to suggest that I went in for penitential practices of any kind. That's a thing, I'm afraid, I've never done; I've heard so much about saintly people who took on the most rigorous mortifications from their childhood upward, but I've never tried to imitate them—the idea never had any attractions for me . . . What I did try to do by way of mortification was to thwart my self-will; . . . to repress the rejoinder which sometimes came to my lips; to do little acts of kindness; . . . to sit upright instead of leaning back in my chair . . . That wasn't much, was it? But I did make these insignificant efforts to make myself less unworthy of a heavenly Bridegroom; and this period of apprenticeship has left tender memories behind it. Three months are soon past" (p. 181).

The most striking aspect of this account of Teresa's preparation for entering Carmel is the depth of her penetration into the mind of Christ. She clearly regarded the external practices of penance as of purely secondary importance. Her aim was above all to learn self-control and to prepare herself inwardly.

Snow: "I forget if I've already mentioned what an attraction snow always had for me; even when I was quite tiny I loved to see the whiteness of it, and took delight in going for a walk when the flakes were falling on me. I wonder what was the reason for it? Perhaps because I was a winter flower myself, and nature was all dressed in white when I first looked out through the eyes of childhood. Anyhow, I'd always hoped that when I dressed in white to take the habit it would be in a white world; and now here was the eve of the great day, and nothing to be seen but a gray sky and a drizzle of rain" (pp. 190–91).

Another beautiful day spoiled—but is it so very important to have snow when one takes the habit?

Jesus's plaything: One day, Teresa writes, "It was borne

in upon me during my prayer that this eagerness to make my profession was mixed up with a good deal of self-love. After all, I'd given myself over to our Lord for his pleasure, his satisfaction, not mine, and here was I trying to see if I could get him to do my will, not his. Another thing occurred to me too; a bride's got to have a trousseau against her wedding day . . . So I told our Lord: . . . I'm ready to wait just as long as you want me to . . . In the meantime, I'll work hard at trying to make myself a lovely wedding dress . . . and when you see that it's ready, I know quite well that nothing in heaven or earth will prevent you from coming to me, and making me, once and forever, your bride" (pp. 194–95).

This is yet another example of Teresa's profoundly serious intention shining through her childlike way of expressing herself. She reiterates here, in a different form, what she has already said, that she wants to be Jesus's little plaything—giving herself over to him *comme son petit jouet*—for him to do what he likes with her.

The canvas: "If the canvas on which an artist is working could think and speak, it obviously wouldn't be annoyed with the brush that kept on touching and retouching it; and it wouldn't be envious either, because it would know perfectly well that all its beauty came from the artist who held the brush, not from the brush itself. And on the other side, the brush couldn't claim any credit for the masterpiece on which it was at work, because it would know quite well that artists are never at a loss; they are the sort of people who enjoy coming up against difficulties, and find it amusing, sometimes, to make use of shoddy and imperfect instruments.

"Well, I'm the poor little brush Jesus has picked out to be the means of imprinting his image on the souls which you have entrusted to me. An artist isn't content to work with one brush, he'll need at least two; there's the really valuable one which he sketches in the general color scheme, covering the whole canvas in no time, and then there's the tiny one which fills in the details . . . I'm the little tiny brush which Jesus uses afterward, to put in the extra flourishes" (p. 280).

Teresa tried in this way to put her mind at rest when she noticed that God was accomplishing great things in others' souls through her. There was, of course, no reason for her to do this, because no one really believed that she was able to do anything extraordinary.

Flight: "In the last resort . . . my recipe for victory is to run away; I used to try this even in my novitiate, and I always found it worked . . . I have a strong feeling that it's better best not to engage in a battle when defeat is quite certain . . . When I look back at my novitiate, . . . it makes me laugh now, to think what heavy weather I made over nothing at all . . . At least I've learned not to be surprised at anything—it doesn't worry me to discover that I am frailty itself; on the contrary, I go about boasting of it. Every day, I expect to find out a fresh lot of imperfections in my character" (pp. 269–70).

Surely this is a totally honest attitude toward Jesus which nothing can disguise or obscure. To conclude our meditation on the spirituality of Teresa, however, we must turn to the great image which she made well known and which made her well known—the image of the lift.

The lift: "As you know, dear Mother, I've always

wished that I could be a saint. But whenever I compared myself to the saints there was always a difference . . . However, I wasn't going to be discouraged; I said to myself: 'God wouldn't inspire us with ambitions that can't be realized. Obviously there's nothing great to be made of me, so it must be possible for me to aspire to sanctity in spite of my insignificance. I've got to take myself just as I am, with all my imperfections; but somehow I shall have to find out a little way, all of my own, which will be a direct shortcut to heaven. After all (I said to myself) we live in an age of inventions. Nowadays, people don't even bother to climb the stairs—rich people, anyhow; they find a lift more convenient. Can't I find a lift which will take me up to Jesus, since I'm not big enough to climb the steep stairway of perfection?' So I looked in the Bible for some hint about the lift I wanted, and I came across the passage where Eternal Wisdom says: 'Is anyone as simple as a child? Then let him come to me.' To that Wisdom I went; it seemed as if I was on the right track; what did God undertake to do for the childlike soul that responded to his invitation? I read on, and this is what I found: 'I will console you like a mother caressing her son; you shall be like children carried at the breast, fondled on a mother's lap'" (pp. 248–49).

I do not think that this passage, the last of my quotations from Teresa of Lisieux, needs any comment.

What can I say in conclusion about this simple woman who died so young? All her life, she lived full of love for God made man, the child Jesus. She knew that this God was love and she sacrificed herself to that love, not as a sacrifice of righteousness, but simply to bear witness.

Combes has observed that, as a witness to God's love, she constantly repeated the message: "Do not be mistaken—our God is not severe. He has no intention. He will not repay evil with evil. Our God is infinite love and overcomes all weakness." This is, of course, the message of Jesus's birth. It is also a promise.

GOD'S BIRTH IN US

God's birth in us

I would like to consider a very simple idea to which John Tauler drew attention as long ago as the fourteenth century—the threefold birth of Christ. In reflecting about these three aspects of Christ's birth, we shall be extending our meditation to its cosmic dimensions. Tauler thought of the three traditional masses of Christmas Day as representing three elements—Christ's birth in the Trinity, his birth in history and his birth in us. Let us think about each of these elements in turn.

Christ's birth in the Trinity

This birth is celebrated at midnight and the mass begins with the words: "The Lord said to me: 'You are my son, today I have begotten you'" (Ps. 2:7). This first mass points to the hidden birth of the Son of God which took place in the Trinity. If we really want to fathom the profound mystery of the birth of Jesus, we must first consider this mystery of mysteries, the eternal process of the Trinity. God, revelation tells us, is three in one. He is a process in which he personally confronts himself and so loves the one who is opposite him, his Son, that his love is a person, the Holy Spirit. God is therefore eternally coming into being, eternally as the witness, the Father, eternally proceeding, as the Son, and eternally as circling love, the Holy Spirit. As creatures, we are intimately connected with this process of the Trinity. By bearing the features of the second person of the Trinity, by living, feeling and thinking, we who are created fulfill the life of God himself in a mysterious way in the world. Our resemblance to Jesus is such that we men, really living and the recipients of grace, are the temples of the Holy Spirit. Living the Christian life and praying as Christians in the world, our aim is to experience that world as the vehicle and dwelling place of God.

Christ's birth in history

The second mass opens with the words: "Today a light will shine upon us" (Isa. 9:2). The Son of God became man one night two thousand years ago in a little village called Bethlehem. He was laid in a manger and wrapped in swaddling clothes. His mother nursed him. He was like all babies, a tiny helpless thing. He shared our human fate entirely. He grew up, almost unnoticed and misunderstood. He encountered hostility everywhere and led a wretched life, surrounded by unimportant people, imprisoned, so to speak, inside a wall of misunderstanding. Our God was very small—the very smallness and unimportance of our God is a great mystery. Christ made humility a fundamental law of the new creation. This is the great mystery of Christmas which was made known in Bethlehem two thousand years ago.

Christ's birth in us

The third mass begins in the day: "For to us a child is born; to us a son is given" (Isa. 9:6). This symbolizes the birth that takes place every day in each one of us.

In her book, *The Envoy of Divine Love,* Gertrude the Great wrote: "One day, I entered the courtyard, sat down by the fishpond and considered the sweetness of the place. The limpidity of the flowing water, the green of the trees, the flight of the birds and of the doves in particular and above all the peacefulness of the place filled me with delight. I began to wonder what could be added to this place to make its joy complete.

"I must have a friend, I thought, a devoted and familiar friend, to make my loneliness sweet. You, my God, drew my thoughts to you. Certainly it was you who inspired me with them. You showed me that my heart could be a dwelling place for you. Like this flowing water, I must be thankful for what you have suggested to me and direct the flow of my thoughts back to you. Like these trees, flourishing in the green of good works, I must increase in strength and devote myself to good works. Like these doves flying, I must raise myself toward heaven . . . In this way, my heart will provide you with a dwelling that is sweeter than any sweetness.

"The whole day long, my mind was full of this idea. In the evening, before I went to bed, when I kneeled to pray, I thought suddenly of the words of Scripture: 'If a man loves me, he will keep my word, and my Father will love him, and we will come to him and make our home with him.' Then I felt in my heart that you had come."

Being a Christian means growing together with Christ. In the words of the Father of the Church: "God became man so that man might become God." The essence of God's becoming man was his emptying of himself. Every Christian is bound at some time or other in his life to come to the point where he is called to be humble and empty himself. He must at that point make his decision, and the real Christian decides to surrender completely and to live for the rest of his life in a spirit of self-surrender.

We realize the attitude of Jesus in our lives by leaving ourselves behind us in selfless love and service of others. He gives us heaven because, in the form of our brother, he was hungry and we gave him food, he was thirsty and we gave him drink, he was a stranger and we welcomed him, he was naked and we clothed him, he was sick and we visited him, he was in prison and we came to him (Matt. 25:35–36). It would seem as though God had forgotten himself in his description of heaven and the judgment, because he appears only in the face of our neighbor. In heaven, what began in the Trinity, continued at Bethlehem and has been realized throughout the history of Christian life will be fully revealed.

In this way, Jesus prepares for his second and last coming in glory. This last Christmas in the world will continue in eternity. It is known as heaven.

BECOMING MAN

Becoming man

"For us men and for our salvation he came down from heaven." This is the answer given by the creed to the old question of Christology: "Why did God become man?" Two reasons are provided in this answer. The first is that he became man "for us men," in other words, so that man can really be himself, that is, man. The second reason is that God became man "for our salvation": in other words, so that he might redeem us from guilt. These are Jesus's two basic functions in the history of man's salvation. They are, however, not equal in value and this difference is expressed in order in which these two reasons are stated in the creed.

God became man in the first place to complete, in Christ, our humanity. Even if sin had not come into the world, Jesus would still have become man, but since man did in fact incur guilt (in other words, since he placed a distance between himself and God), Jesus first "had to" reconcile us with God and become our redeemer. This second and subsequent function does not, however, cancel the primary reason for his becoming man, the act that had been foreseen and planned from the very beginning. Although he saved us from sin, he is above all the one who enables us to become fully and really human. This fulfillment of our humanity took place finally on the cross.

Jesus raises our humanity—and therefore also the universe, which is concentrated in us—up to the level of completion. In this sense, he is the God who lifts up. The ultimate statement that can be made about God, a statement which represents an absolute limit to human thought, is "God became man." Anything that we can say, feel or do pales into insignificance beside this statement. Any attempt to fathom it reveals how fragile human thought is. It is a statement that is frequently repeated, but we ought to be extremely careful when we make it, as careful as God himself, whose preparation for the incarnation took so long and who allowed this statement, "God became man," to rise up very slowly and gently from the whole of man's experience.

What would have become of us if God were not so patient, if he did not let everything come to maturity with such gentle and attentive restraint? God is very forbearing with man, with the whole of his existence including his thinking. He is eternal and is neither fearful nor in a hurry. He knows how vulnerable we are and so he does not force us, intimidate us, or press us. He stands quietly at our door and knocks very gently.

In this meditation, we should approach the mystery of God's incarnation from a point of view which is based on our experience as men, which we can discuss easily and which does not confuse us. For our point of departure, we can take Paul's statement: "All things are yours, and you are Christ's, and Christ is God's" (1 Cor. 3:22–23). If we consider this text very attentively, we may be able to come closer to the heart of the ultimate mystery: that in Christ the world is completed and brought to fulfillment.

All things are yours. The incarnation of the world

One of the most striking aspects of present-day thinking is its emphasis on man's increasing awareness of his intimate connection with the world. He no longer regards the world as a static factor or as a framework that is already given and unchanging. On the contrary, he sees it as an evolving process, a continuing development, something that is still in the course of becoming. He is aware of the continued formation, for example, of the Milky Way, the solar system and the planets, of the production of increasingly complicated forms of life and of a tentative movement forward and upward to a higher level of existence and consciousness.

Man knows that he is closely linked to this world and regards himself as the product of an evolution that has lasted for many millions of years, but also as the summit of this evolutionary effort in the world. The universe ("all things") is, as it were, dwelling within him. The place where man is most radically connected with the universe is his body. In and through the human body the world changes into the spiritual, so that the human body is also the place of change, in which the matter of the world is united with the spirit. The essential aspect of the spirit, however, is that it is infinitely open to the infinite. This radical transformation of the material into the spiritual is known simply as "man," who is spirit become body or body become spirit. This means that man is the center of the universe, of "all things." All the material forces of the world are concentrated in him and these forces thrust forward in him into the spiritual sphere. Man is the highest unit of evolution in the world, combining in perfect unity body and spirit.

According to Christian thought, which reached one of its highest points in the theology of Thomas Aquinas, man is a unified being. In man, spirit and matter are essentially one. Man is not composed of two separate, "things," spirit and matter—he is one single being. From these two closely united factors comes a third which is neither one nor the other, the soul. The human soul is the highest development of the body. The teaching of Thomas Aquinas about the unity of the body and the soul enables us to gain some insight into man's intimate connection with the world which we mentioned at the beginning of this section. This relationship between the body and the soul makes it possible for the universe to enter fully into the openness of the spirit. The human body, the product of an evolutionary process that has taken millions of years in the world, is really spirit. It is not simply that man's body shelters or contains spirit—spirit is inherent in man's body and essentially one with it.

The evolution of the universe reveals a distinct preference for more unified and more complex forms. This tendency is even clearer in the higher stages of evolution and it is in man that the world finally achieves its distinctive character of spirit. In this sense, then, the evolutionary process is the birth of man. This incarnation of the world has taken place since the very beginning of the development of the cosmos.

This cosmic incarnation must be seen everywhere, in each one of its phases, not simply in the creation of the human soul, as real creation. This arises from the very concept of evolution itself. Evolution, after all, means that a more develops from a less, that the world surpasses itself in its being. This is something that is happening not simply here and there and at certain times, but at every moment of the entire process of development. It would be quite wrong to think that God intervened again and again in his creation, as though the world were a machine which God tunes up to higher and higher performance in the course of time. On the contrary, the world itself develops—God does not develop the world. He is outside the chain of cause and effect in the world and is not a link in the chain of second causes. He creates the world by giving it the forces to create itself, to raise its level of being even higher and to evolve toward the spirit. In this sense, then, the world itself can be said to produce the human spirit in a process which does not in any way throw doubt on the creation by God of each individual human soul. Body and soul, we are completely children of this earth and in this we are also completely children of God.

We may, however, go a stage further and say that, as children of this earth, we already have God's life in us. To say simply that God creates us out of nothing is to define negatively God's creative activity. God's creation of man from himself, however, according to no law other than his own and under no influence but his own, is the postive aspect of that work of creation. All creation lives, in other words, as the thought and image of God. In this way, all creation is mysteriously but intimately connected with the second person of the Trinity. The Logos is the perfect expression of the first person of the Trinity, the Father, an image confronting the Father who is the Father himself. It is in this perfect image of God that the possibility of a creation is based, in other words, the possibility of an infinite image or copy of God. Every human is this image in so far as he bears the likeness of the second person of the Trinity.

If we combine this idea with the one outlined previously, that of a continuous creative process seen as evolution, we see that the world proceeds from the second person of the Trinity with creative newness from second to second, that the Logos is present with his creative activity at every point in the evolutionary process, creating his own image in the world. We may say, in other words, that the Son gives the world the ability to get along on its own, to use its own forces to work its way upward toward him, "for in him all things were created" (Col. 1:16) and "all things were created through him and for him" (Col. 1:7). The temporary but real aim of the cosmic process is man. After a long period of tentative seeking, the evolutionary process of creation finds its ultimate form. A breach was at last made in matter when the human spirit was produced in the world and this has caused the biological forces of change to become gradually less powerful. With every year, every month and every hour, the spirit is created more and more in the world, with the result that knowledge, love, and freedom are constantly increasing with the passage of time.

But what does all this mean in terms of the Christian's spiritual life in his day-to-day existence? In the first place and above all, it means that he lives in a holy world. It means that he must include the whole world in his Christian life and prayer. It means that he must try to experience Christ in all truth and in all creation. He must have boundless respect for every creature, be attentive to the whole of life, have good intentions for everyone and everything in creation, even the humblest, and be open to all truth, wherever it comes from. This is the first and most important demand imposed on us by this view.

In the second place, however, it means that we must try to understand that our humanity is holy and that we have to behave correspondingly toward our fellow men. Yet, while thinking of other people, we should not forget that we too are holy and that we must accept ourselves with all our limitations and weariness and with the desires and promises that are constantly breaking through our limitations. We have also to accept that we are what we have become, because it is from our concrete existence here and now that we have set out in search of God. This is not something that can simply be taken for granted. Our fellow men are holy and we must also honor and respect their holiness, recognize their distinctiveness, never violate their freedom, defend them if they are insignificant, vulnerable or helpless. In short, we must be polite toward each other, bearing constantly in mind that politeness includes consideration and deep sympathy for the other person's life, his difference from ourselves, his circumstances and his difficulties.

Finally and in the third place, it means that we should never be satisfied with what has already been done, with the situation that we have already reached. We must allow the impulse which has driven the universe to higher and higher stages of being in the evolutionary process and has become finally concentrated in man to go on working powerfully within us. We must therefore not have too exalted a view of ourselves, of our own achievements and structures or even of our own idea of "God." Above all, we must think of God as greater and more all-embracing than all our own imaginings—we must not restrict him to concepts and formulas. We must not delude ourselves into thinking that we have him in our grasp. We should not be mean in our attitude to life—ours and those of others. We have to allow ourselves to be carried by love beyond anything that we or others might achieve.

These three demands of our Christian understanding of creation in the sense of the incarnation of the world point the way to a new dimension of the incarnation. Since the world has been, so to speak, "made man" in us and has produced us body and soul, we have the task of becoming more human. The incarnation is, in other words, not yet complete. The evolution of the world merely produced the matter from which we, through our own efforts, have to fashion ourselves into full men. This is the second aspect of the incarnation.

You are Christ's. The incarnation of man

There are many different paths which man can follow in his quest for completion of fulfillment, so many that it would be impossible for me to discuss them even briefly here. What is important for us to bear in mind in this context, however, is that man does not exist in the world in an already finished state—he is, as it were, only a preliminary design of his real self. There is in him a mysterious tension between what he is now and what he ought to be, between what he has already accomplished and what still remains to be achieved. The man who really aims to *be* has to begin again and again anew. This beginning is a constantly effective element in the condition of being man.

What it means is that man must continuously resolve anew to exist as man. To do this, he must, so to speak, be brave enough to be a man, that is, to see dangers and confront them without retreating and to make use of even the most difficult situations in order to grow more and more fully into manhood. He must allow what is really vital and what holds out the greatest promise for his future to emerge from his innermost being. The early Christians called this exertion the "practice of virtue," a phrase which strikes us nowadays as rather antiquated and which makes us feel a little uneasy. But it is, on the contrary, a description which is most meaningful, as anyone who has experienced the bitterness of looking back at his life and realizing that it had not turned out at all as it should have done will admit.

Is it true, however, to say that man can complete himself of his own accord, that he can, by his own effort, fulfill all the possibilities that are present in embryo within him? Fortunately or unfortunately, this is not the case. And this, of course, brings us to the heart of the matter, namely that it is impossible for man to attain the real essence of his being as man, for him to fulfill himself completely as man. Man's being, in other words, infinitely transcends itself.

I should like to develop this idea by analyzing briefly three basic functions of human reality. The first of these is human knowledge. Acting in the sphere of knowledge, the human spirit has the task of appropriating a concrete reality without in any sense violating what is known. We begin to explore the world by gaining knowledge of individual objects and by gradually understanding the relationship between man and other living organisms. We also learn how to deal with these relationships through acquiring knowledge. Increasing knowledge also reveals to us the laws governing nature, human society as a whole and personal relationships generally. The acquisition of isolated fragments or areas of knowledge in this way is undeniably valuable, but we also have to try, despite repeated failure, to relate these separate areas of knowledge to each other and to combine them together in a logically worked out system. In attempting to do this, we inevitably begin to sense the existence of something much more all-embracing which cannot be approached simply by combining together all our individual bits of knowledge.

This experience is sometimes accompanied by an insight into what can only be called the ground of all being, the reality which has so far eluded us and which is clearly capable of transforming the world. Once we have experienced this insight into the ultimate reality, we understand that our thirst for knowledge has always been motivated by something much more than mere curiosity. We become aware that we have already been attracted by an absolute, by the fullness of being. Drawn on by this absolute, we have discovered the concrete and individual things of everyday life, but these have never been able to satisfy our longing. In our quest for separate fragments of knowledge, we have always at the same time wanted to know the God who is completely different. We are therefore always, at least implicitly, in search of God when we are seeking knowledge. In every limited sphere of knowledge, the absolute comes closer to us.

We may, then, conclude that our human knowledge will be completed when the absolute becomes a reality that can be fully grasped and unlimited being is completely contained within a limited being. Until that happens, then, man continues to long for the incarnation of God in every act of knowledge.

The second function is human longing. This is also divided between the unlimited nature of the demands that it makes and the limited extent to which it can be realized. Man is always dissatisfied with any success in the world. A mysterious element within him urges him constantly onward toward new promises, new aims and new achievements. An inexorable necessity drives him on toward something more, but every attempt to fulfill his longing is condemned to failure.

This is why we often, perhaps too often, pause on the way and accept what is temporary as ultimate. This, however, usually results in unhappiness and a sense of unfulfillment, which we may not even admit to ourselves. If we are completely honest, then, we do not try to live without longing, but continue to strive toward the infinite even in our everyday lives.

Throughout history, man has always been drawn by the

unknown, which has seemed to him to be more beautiful than what he already has or knows and therefore worth every effort to reach—and this is still so today. His genesis, in other words, is still in progress and every time he is fulfilled he must at once begin his search again. A taste for happiness, a basic optimism, a hope that he will find even greater fulfillment—these are fundamental to human life. The Apostle Paul was clearly aware that man was driven by his very nature to "walk in newness of life" (Rom. 6:4), but he was also conscious of the burden imposed by this way of life: "So we do not lose heart. Though our outward nature is wasting away, our inner nature is being renewed every day" (2 Cor. 4:16).

This means that man has within him a dynamic tendency toward what is humanly within his grasp: in other words, what is given to him as grace is at the same time what he of necessity wants. It is only possible for his longing to be fulfilled when he is confronted with the object of that longing, when the absolute is completely contained within what can be reached and grasped, in other words, when God becomes man. At the center of all man's longings, then, is God.

This brings us to the third function of the reality of man's existence—human love. Love exists when two persons enter into a unity of being, when they say of that being not "I" but "we." It is a process in which two people live entirely from each other. The ultimate intention of love, however, goes far beyond anything that can be achieved here and now by this love. Love anticipates, in its present form, this ultimate fulfillment and completion. What man is looking for in love is something unconditional, unlimited and infinite which lies beyond what is conditional, limited and finite. Limited love is an impossibility. In our striving toward the infinite, then, we make a fragile, finite being the object of our love. This is a demand that no person can ever fully satisfy, because, however greatly that person is loved, he is not equal to the love that flows toward him.

Love therefore has to struggle every day against the force of the evidence that "you are limited" and in a desperate attempt to attribute an unlimited character to this limitation. Anyone who has ever loved knows that this is the real temptation of human love and that it is this which gives us a certain insight into the meaning of Louis Aragon's poem, "There is no happy love." Human love simply cannot be fulfilled. The absolute therefore has to be present completely in a finite person, so that the real object of man's love is, in other words, God who has become man. Whenever man loves sincerely, his inner intention always includes the incarnate God.

I shall now try to summarize the first two elements, knowledge and longing, and to bring them together. The evolutionary process in the world is transformed in man, living in him in his restless hopes, dreams, and desires as an orientation toward the infinite on the part of a finite creature. This concentration of the whole of evolution in the human reality produces in us an enormous pressure of ideas and desires. A process of fermentation is going on inside us all the time, a process in which the universe is struggling upward in us toward the absolute.

We can therefore understand now how "all things were created for him," how, in other words, all creation and all creative energy is directed toward Jesus Christ. The birth of the Son of God is therefore not an isolated event which took place without reference to the evolution of the universe. On the contrary, the incarnation is the completion of the universe and the fulfillment of man's existence. God as it were had to enter history because he created the world to move toward him. "All things are yours, and you are Christ's." We must now consider the third statement made in this text:

Christ is God's. The incarnation of God

Now that we have prepared the way for an understanding of the almost incomprehensible event of the incarnation by approaching it as far as possible from the vantage point of our own experience, we can at last pronounce that most mysterious of all sentences: God became man. As we have seen, nothing is more reasonable than this statement. Without it, the whole world and the whole human reality would be unthinkable. But our task now is to make a supreme effort and try to understand the tremendous nature of what we have been discussing so far. The best approach may be to analyze briefly the three elements of this statement in turn: "God," "God becomes," and "God becomes man."

Firstly, *God*. Man cannot grasp or understand this name, which stands for something that is far beyond him. Thinking about God, he is tempted simply to bring together everything that he knows in the world and above all in himself, everything that is beautiful and exalted, all his longings and the fulfillment of all his desires, in other words, all that is best in him and regard this as "God." The temptation, then, is to worship himself and in this way to destroy everything, since he can never fulfill his longings, which must always be beyond his reach. God can never be thought of as composed of anything that is found in this world. Man can only be fulfilled by what is completely different. He can only speak about this fulfillment if he denies, in the same breath, what has just been said. It may be that our profound experience of God nowadays as the completely different one is a sign of very special grace. It is also possible that man has to endure this terrible experience of God's being very far away so that he may begin to feel how radically different God really is.

Secondly, *God becomes*. If we believe that the most sublime and the most pure thoughts can be expressed about God, then we seem bound also to say that God cannot become. He is the one who infinitely is above all change and all passing away. He is the "unmoved mover" who is self-sufficient and dependent on nobody. That is a very exalted and beautiful concept of God, but it is fundamentally wrong. It is true that we cannot think of God in any other way, yet he *is* different in fact. How is he different from the concept? How can he be known as the one who is not simply completely different and far from us?

It is, of course, in the light of his revelation of himself at Christmas that we experience him not only as completely different from ourselves, but as like us, not only as distant, but at the same time as near to us. Our God has appeared to us—"Philip, he who has seen me has seen the Father" (John 14:9). The God of revelation comes and goes. He prepares his coming with great care and after he has come to us he goes away from us, tearing himself, as it were, from us. He becomes a little child, lives inconspicuously among us, learns how to be a carpenter, travels around a good deal, becomes tired, even exhausted and completes his work afraid, sweating blood and crying out that God has forsaken him. The idea of a static and exalted God may be difficult for us to grasp, but that of a God who becomes is totally bewildering. Our bewilderment is increased as soon as we begin to consider the third element in the statement:

God becomes man. It is a strange fact that, although we long with all our being for God's presence, as soon as he comes to us, we can no longer endure it. There are many examples of this in the Bible—man's encounter with God in his revelation of himself is painful and brings about a revolution in his life. When God appears, man must hide his face. He falls as though dead. He conceals himself from God, as our earliest ancestors did in a profoundly symbolic gesture. "Whither shall I flee from thy presence?" the psalmist cried, "If I ascend to heaven, thou art there! If I make my bed in Sheol, thou art there!" (Ps. 139:7–8). A stranger looks unflinchingly at us and, like Job, we cry out: "How long wilt thou not look away from me, nor let me alone till I swallow my spittle?" (Job 7:19). At Sinai, the frightened people of Israel beseeched Moses: "You speak to us and we will hear, but let not God speak to us, lest we die" (Exod. 20:20).

In his incarnation, however, God breaks through this experience. He appears as a child, helpless in the crib and needing the love and care of his people, his creatures. He no longer threatens man, but appeals to him. Just before Jesus's appearance, John the Baptist spoke threateningly about what Christ would do when he came, but in fact he proved to be a man who was full of goodness and understanding who defended sinners and weak people not only from other people, but even from his Father. Christ stood up for us, so completely that Paul was able to say: "If we are faithless, he remains faithful, for he cannot deny himself" (2 Tim. 2:13). From the time of Christ's coming, it has been impossible to think of anything that is human—apart from sin—which is not at the same time applicable to God. Christ transformed God's power into grace and goodness.

The God of the incarnation, then, is both infinitely far and infinitely near, both incomprehensibly different from us and yet very similar to us. All that is good and beautiful in the world is present in him and yet all this goes far beyond any possible fulfillment on earth and enters his life, the life of God. From now on, there is only one event in the world—the mysterious birth of Christ; and this is the real meaning of Christmas for us today, because the shepherds are no longer out in the field and the child Jesus is no longer in his crib in Bethlehem. That all happened in the past. One thing, however, remains today Christ's birth in humanity, the birth of the "cosmic" Christ.

One of the most profound insights in the whole of Paul's teaching is that, although Christ really came in history, he is still coming and will continue to come until the end of the world. Christ's birth takes place throughout the whole of history and at the end of time there will be the fullness of Christ, the *plerōma*. Christians build up his body. That is their Christmas in the world. It is also the meaning of the sacraments and of the whole of the Christian way of life. In their lives, Christians—both those who profess their faith publicly and those whose Christianity is anonymous—enter into Christ and build him up. When the measure of Christ is full, when all those comprise the fullness of Christ's being have grown up into him, the "cosmic" Christ will have been born, heaven will be present and the first creation will be complete. It is then that life will really begin and that the extraordinary adventure of the world will end.

What does all this mean for us in our lives here and now? It means that we should live in such a way that we go beyond our limitations and enter the sphere that is beyond our understanding. We must accept that our dissatisfaction is inspired by God and that we must again and again overcome the narrowness of our existence. God has created us for himself and we are bound to be restless until we have found him, the infinite one.

Nothing is great enough for man, weak though he is. To be human is a breath-taking experience. God is constantly drawing us onward out of our habits and our narrow, small life. If we remain satisfied with what we have already achieved, we are clearly not being as God intended us to be. How, then, can we be completely open to the absolute? Simply by being each other's brothers and loving and serving our fellow men in our everyday lives. "As you did it to one of the least of these my brethren, you did it to me" (Matt. 25:40). This is the greatest and most profound aspect of the mystery of Jesus's birth.

INCALCULABLE GOD

Incalculable God

At the time of Jesus's birth, we again become aware of the fact that God is different, that he has no habits, that his ways are always new, that he is young and that, when he comes to us, it is in the way that he chooses. Christmas is therefore the feast of the incalculable God. But it is not only then that he is incalculable. Even later, after his resurrection, he appeared quite surprisingly as a gardener, as a hungry traveler and as a man on the shore of the lake: on each occasion as someone who could be mistaken for somebody else.

God comes unexpectedly and when he comes he is always different. His ways can never be calculated in advance. This can be a threat to the man who is looking for him. How bold and uninhibited must have been the faith of the men who first kneeled in the straw and worshiped God in the child they found at Bethlehem. This thought, that God is incalculable, gives us a suitable point of departure for a meditation on a theme that is hardly ever considered seriously or, if it is considered at all, is only mentioned incidentally—the theme of the temptations of Christmas.

The first temptation is that God cannot be tied down. Because he is so incalculable, man can never have him in his power. He can never hold God or do what he wants with him. He always eludes man's grasp. He cannot be bound by rules, systems, or methods. Even the saints fell into this trap sometimes; they tried again and again to coerce God with a great number of prayers, numerous provisos, and long hours of contemplation. They longed to have him, his word and his revelation wholly at their disposal all the time, and to experience his grace and his consolation constantly. But God taught them a better way.

It was right for man to prepare the way for God, to lift up every valley and to make low every mountain and hill, by prayer, by conquering his self-will and above all simply by living well every day of his life. But it was entirely up to God whether he chose to walk along the way prepared for him, or whether he preferred a different way; whether he wanted to enter by the door that had been decorated so festively for him, or whether he went in by another door altogether. We are therefore bound to conclude that the only real attitude that the saint can have is simply to be ready and available, to persist, to open his soul to God and to spread out his arms to receive him. God will be present for him when and where and in whatever way God pleases.

Paul expresses this question of man's relationship with God in incomprehensible terms in his Letter to the Romans: "I will have mercy on whom I have mercy, and I will have compassion on whom I have compassion. So it depends not upon man's will or exertion, but upon God's mercy" (Rom. 9:15–16). The same attitude emerges in a most impressive way from Psalm 127: "Unless the Lord builds the house, those who build it labor in vain. Unless the Lord watches over the city, the watchman stays awake in vain. It is in vain that you rise up early and go late to rest, eating the bread of anxious toil; for he gives to his beloved sleep."

The best way to prepare for God's coming unexpectedly into our lives is by silence. This is why, in the Christmas liturgy, we sing: "While all things were in quiet silence, and that night was in the midst of its swift course, thy almighty word leaped down from heaven out of the royal throne" (Wis. 18:14–15). The Apostolic Father, Ignatius, Bishop of Antioch, called Christ, in his letter to the Magnesians, "the Word proceeded from silence." Even those who were not believers had some inkling of this connection between God's presence and silence. Heraclitus, for example, maintained that the authentic attitude of the spirit was one of "listening quietly to the truth of things," a silence before the mystery. It is in silence that we experience the constant newness of God. We prepare ourselves best for his incalculable ways when we are silent.

The second temptation of Christmas is that God often disappoints us. How is this little child to keep his hands firmly on the reins and curb the world? It would seem, however, that God is weak and helpless in all his government of the world. He is not bright, wonderful, or powerful enough for us. Why does his strength not shine out more clearly? Why does he spare evil men and let men of good will be sacrificed? Why does he allow so much effort to be wasted? Why does he let so much half-finished work go to ruin and everything be begun again? Apparently he isn't a match for the world.

On the other hand, we should not forget that we are always inclined to be disappointed by what we have come to value and love most of all. The ultimate reality lacks the concentrated availability of what is in the foreground of our experience. We can hardly expect what strikes us as bright and wonderful to make the same impression on everyone; this is often a painful experience. At the same time, even the holiest people sometimes have doubts about what or whom they love most of all—their wife, mother, friend, or God. But if we undertake the most important task of all for the Christian, and try to overcome this temptation to disappointment, we are bound to discover that the ultimate reality cannot be demonstrated and that it can appear only as our surrender of ourselves gets closer to perfection. We cannot expect the object of our love to be loved equally by all people. There is an ultimate point in man at which the gift is unique and individual: something valid only for that one man.

Our attempt to overcome this temptation to be disappointed by God will gradually result in a deeper spiritual experience of the world around us, and a disclosure of the essential elements beneath the superficial features that can be seen and understood by all men. This temptation to be disappointed is undoubtedly a phase through which we must all pass on our way toward the ultimate reality of God.

The third temptation is that God directs us back to our everyday lives. He did this by becoming a child and subjecting himself to ordinary simple people. True religiousness and pride cannot co-exist in the same person. Man's spirit is made more sensitive, more all-embracing and more translucent when his experience of faith is authentic. The limits of his own being are extended and a peak is reached in his own existence which is at the same time a culminating point in the world. In spirit, he floats above a bright abyss and the whole world seems, at times like this, to be small and insignificant. His spirit transcends the world and enters a completely different and unknown sphere. A feeling of strength and greatness overcomes him.

But sooner or later the Christian has to return from this heightened experience and descend to the world of everyday life inhabited by ordinary, even miserable people —the world to which he is called by the God who became man, who became a little child. In this sense, Jesus's birth brought about a revolution in man's religious attitudes, making complete forgetfulness of one's own greatness and the overcoming of one's own pride the condition of true greatness. Since the Christ-event, greatness has only taken up its habitation in men who know that they are nothing and who have repudiated their own glory. Since Jesus's birth, there has been a close and indeed unbreakable connection between the renunciation of greatness and true human greatness, in other words, between sacrifice and joy. What took place when a certain Jewish mother gave life to her child appears contradictory, because it is difficult to accept that sacrifice and joy can be one, that we can only enrich our lives by giving away and that we must renounce if we are to become really great. This contradiction is, after all, a truth that can never be proved—it can only be experienced.

The most powerful of all temptations that can assail the Christian is that the ultimate ground of the human reality can never be verified in this life. It is only if we endure this temptation until the end of our life that we can begin to understand that "whoever exalts himself will be humbled, and whoever humbles himself will be exalted" (Matt. 23:12; Luke 14:11). It is almost impossible to express these extremely delicate aspects of the human heart in really fitting words. The Magnificat, the song of Mary which is the most appropriate of all Christmas songs, expresses this idea very beautifully: "He has shown strength with his arm, he has scattered the proud in the imagination of their hearts, he has put down the mighty from their thrones, and exalted those of low degree; he has filled the hungry with good things, and the rich he has sent empty away" (Luke 1:51–53). Anyone who did not know where this song came from would perhaps think that it was a revolutionary song. In fact, it really is a song of the revolution—the revolution of Christmas.

The spirit of the incarnation can be expressed quite simply as: "Though he was in the form of God, he did not count equality with God a thing to be grasped, but emptied himself, taking the form of a servant, being born in the likeness of men. And being found in human form he humbled himself and became obedient unto death, even death on a cross" (Phil. 2:6–8). This shows us that the prior condition of becoming a Christian is to empty oneself, to become completely selfless. Man finds his innermost reality by giving himself completely. By giving himself away, he at the same time preserves himself, completes himself and reaches fulfillment. He can only keep himself in this way, paradoxically, if he loosens his grip on himself. Human nature is essentially oriented toward an ecstasy—man must stand outside himself and reveal himself in order to find himself. The more he clings to himself, the less human he becomes.

The spirit of Jesus's incarnation is therefore the spirit of man's incarnation. If man locks himself up inside his own self, he will remain without promise. We may therefore say that, in the last resort, the process by which man becomes himself, his incarnation, includes death. (And this also applies to Jesus's incarnation, of course.) It is, moreover, in death that man is so completely taken away from himself that, if he gives his free consent to being taken away from himself in this way, he will be capable of being completely humble; that is, that he will, by giving himself away completely, be able to fulfill his humanity. That is why Paul regards Jesus's incarnation as "obedience unto death." But in the mind of the Christian death immediately evokes the idea of resurrection: in the light of the incarnation, the way of the God who became a child is clearly revealed as the way of the God who died and rose again. The burden of Christmas is unutterably heavy, but its promise is very bright.

God created an entirely new order by becoming man: an order in which man can be completed and fulfilled by freely consenting to be small and insignificant. He has caught us up in a vital movement of self-detachment which, if we accept death, will lead to resurrection. To do that, he has had to overturn all our systems and all our ideas. He has had to expose us to the dangers involved in his being incalculable, disappointing us, and showing us the way back to everyday life; because only if we accept these dangers can we overcome our enclosure within ourselves and move toward our ultimate fulfillment.

One last point: Even if we have fully understood all this and taken in the message of Jesus's birth, we should not think for a moment that we have grasped the ultimate truth, or that the essence of it all has really taken hold of us. We have done no more than reach the end of one stage of our unending advance into the mystery. Our conception of it is simply the beginning of an even greater understanding. All that we do is to drive furiously after God, without ever catching him up or overtaking him. On our earthly level of existence this may seem very distressing; in fact it is the precondition for boundless happiness: the joy of seeking God.

* * *

The journey of the wise men from the East to Bethlehem symbolizes our existence here on earth and our ultimate fulfillment as human beings. We look for God, in order to find him, during our life on earth. We look for God, after we have found him, in eternal happiness.

So that men will continue to look for him in order to find him, God remains boundless, immeasurable, infinite. That is the structure of the creature's becoming God, a form of becoming that of its nature is never completed.

In this spirit, too, we kneel down in silence before the mystery of the God who became a little child. Perhaps, like the wise men from the East, we will be told to go back "by another way" to our own country; in other words, back to the everyday world. Anyone who has once been seized by this God and has beheld his salvation has already begun a new life along entirely new ways.

GUILTY, O LORD

GUILTY, O LORD

Yes, I still go to confession

Bernard Basset, S.J.

Doubleday & Company, Inc., Garden City, New York
1975

This book was originally published in England by Sheed and Ward, Ltd. under the title *Guilty, My Lord*

Nihil obstat: F. J. Bartlett, Censor. *Imprimatur:* David Norris, Vicar General Westminster, October 15, 1973

Library of Congress Cataloging in Publication Data

Basset, Bernard.
Guilty, O Lord; yes, I still go to confession.

British ed. published under title: Guilty, my Lord.
1. Confession. I. Title.
BX2265.2.B323 1975 234′.166
ISBN 0-385-02531-9
Library of Congress Catalog Card Number 74–9475

To the memory
of my dear brother
Fr. Edmund Basset, S.J.
who died in May

Contents

GUILTY, O LORD

1. Guilty, O Lord

Here is a breezy book on a somber subject, the confession and forgiveness of sin. Any such book must be cheerful for few happier experiences than forgiveness are known to man. With what relief we owned up in childhood, no matter how angry our loving parents pretended to be. After a tissue of lies and false pretenses, it was a joy to be both wicked and free. One of St. Thomas More's daughters admitted later that she used to be deliberately naughty for the very pleasure of being forgiven by him.

The child is father of the man. As we grow older confession and forgiveness may not be so simple but they are twice as sweet. In the case of lovers, nothing promotes the match better than the tearful reconciliation after a trivial tiff. Every happy marriage is a mosaic of mistakes, sorrow and forgiveness, every understanding friendship implies just this. Dorothy Sayers put this well. "Forgiveness is not a doing-away with consequences; nor is it, primarily, a remission of punishment. A child may be forgiven and 'let off' punishment or punished and then forgiven, either way may bring good results. But no good will come of leaving him unpunished and unforgiven. Forgiveness is the re-establishment of a right relationship in which the parties can genuinely feel and behave as freely with one another as though the unhappy incident had never taken place."[1]

If confession and forgiveness are essential in human relations, they are of infinite importance in man's relationship with God. Wherever man has existed, sin has flourished and sin leads to sorrow and that yearning for forgiveness, so central a theme in the New Testament and in the Old. The subject is far wider than the Bible for if, in length, it takes us back to Adam, in width it embraces all the four corners of the earth. I have been reading about the potential liturgies in ancient Greece, India, Tibet, Peru. One of the problems in a book on such a subject must be the vastness of the area to be covered and its complexity.

Happily, my book has a practical purpose which need not involve us in the penitential rites of ancient Peru.[2] The need for confession and forgiveness is basic to human nature and we may examine this in the context of the Christian faith. Though we thus reduce the subject, it still remains vast.

In Christian literature there are books upon books dealing with sin, sorrow, and forgiveness from a legal point of view. These tell us about mortal and venial sin, lay down the laws governing confession and the formulas to be used. On other shelves in the library, the theology of sin and forgiveness is treated, involving us in the whole story of the incarnation down to Christ's death on the cross. Then there are the apologetic books in which the practice of confession is defended in a hostile world. On these shelves we might find the works of Luther, Calvin, Zwingli, St. John Fisher and St. Thomas More. Nor should we ignore the pious books about confession, sometimes irreverently called "the tear-jerkers," sermons by great revivalists with John Bunyan in the van. Some of these aspects of sin and forgiveness may be touched on later but none are essential to my theme. It is the psychology of sin and forgiveness which most concerns me at the moment and this is an approach not often treated in books.

The sacrament of penance is under great pressure at the moment, in a changing world. Conflicting theories, criticisms, practices are causing much confusion and not a little misery. There are those who loved the old dispensation and resent all changes and those whose faith in the sacrament is fast fading away. I am a middle-of-the-roader, happy but mildly apprehensive; too many babies have been thrown out with the bath water in these progressive days.

In a period of drift and confusion, it has seemed to me important to re-examine both sides of the question and then to make up my mind for myself. One must sift the essentials from the nonessentials, accept changes but, even in pontifical circles, count one's change.

Though my views about confession have expanded and deepened, I look back to the practices of childhood days with affection, not regret. Along with many of you, I took confession for granted from my tenderest years. I made my first confession at the age of six in Westminster Cathedral, fifty-eight years ago. They told me only after it was over that the ancient Monsignor who absolved me was stone deaf.

As child, schoolboy, student I liked confessing my sins. It cost nothing and gave me the kind of gesture of sorrow that I wanted to make. Later in life, I would witness the "childrens' confessions" in large city parishes, during which the Church would be transformed into a battlefield or marketplace. Hitler, who confessed as a child in similar conditions, once described the pandemonium. No pressure was exerted in my schooldays to get us into the box.

The situation altered slightly after I became a priest. Priests, also, need forgiveness and must practice what they preach. In many ways, confession is more irksome for a priest. For him, it often means a special journey to dig out a colleague who knows him well. If his sins are small he feels foolish thus to disturb his neighbor, if large, he feels ashamed of himself. Happily, among priests, confession is a routine business with an unemotional approach. Looking back, I chuckle at an incident in Boston some eighteen years ago. Having just arrived from Britain, I tracked down an ancient Jesuit to his room. Boston was roasting in a heat wave; I found my confessor relaxing in his rocking chair and reading the psalms of David in the nude. I turned towards the door, embarrassed, but he said blandly, "Confession, Father: be kind enough to pass me my stole."

It just so happens that I am writing about confession at a moment in life when I cannot get to confession easily. Living as I do on the Isles of Scilly, out in the East Atlantic, the sacrament would cost me a flight by helicopter to Penzance. No sin that I commit on these simple islands is worth £7.

Over my years as a priest, the reality of sin and the joy of receiving absolution has been brought home to me in three different ways. The experience which opens one's eyes to the psychology of forgiveness is the assisting of a patient who is going to die. In such situations, the personality of the priest counts for very little, it is forgiveness that the dying man yearns for and which brings with it an overwhelming relief. I saw with my own two eyes both sorrow and happiness visible on a human face. On more routine occasions, the sacrament may sometimes appear banal and boring; in the final crisis one experiences the bond between happiness and faith.

Were I to pretend that my life had been spent ministering to the dying, I would have to catch the next helicopter to Penzance. Certainly the experience of hearing a last confession is deeply rewarding to any priest. For me there has been a second revelation of the power of forgiveness during the thirty years in which I have directed retreats. A retreat is more than a series of talks or a casual conference: it is a valid form of spiritual therapy. During retreats, the director spends the best part of the day listening to the problems and worries of many people, some of whom are facing agonizing situations with courage which he cannot claim himself.

This second experience of the power of forgiveness differs slightly from that known when attending a patient at death. While listening to the troubles of the living, one comes across the ravages caused by a sense of guilt. Oddly enough, the dying move into a sphere which is out of reach of guilt. Just as a patient in hospital achieves peace by surrendering to the doctors, so the dying man recovers his equilibrium when he commits himself entirely, with all his sins, to God. No firm purpose of amendment is required at the time of death. Those suffer guilt who must go home and reach decisions not required by the pilgrim at the journey's end.

I must have directed retreats for tens of thousands over these thirty years. Such statistics do not prove me holy, only that I know a thing or two. Nor are retreatants all retired ladies or maidens crossed in love. Almost my first retreat was given in wartime Britain to seventy Royal Air Force personnel. My last, three months ago, was to sixty assorted farmers in Pineville, Louisiana. To this retreat one client brought his tape recorder but not to flatter me. A poultry farmer with sixty thousand hens, he could not face two nights without them; a tape played quietly in the early morning saved him from melancholy.

The third experience which so greatly helped and surprised me has been the desperate need of so many to get things off their chest. The satisfaction of owning up, which so many of us knew in childhood, quickly becomes a habit and persists.

Doctors, lawyers, nurses, priests, even policemen are well aware of this.

Such an experience as this contradicts the popular impression that men and women dislike confessing their sins. They may find the ritual irksome or the confessional box offputting but the desire to tell someone of their behavior proves a built-in safety valve. I have seen this in hospital with patients—of no religion and total strangers—who will grab an opportunity to speak about their sins. One saw the same with soldiers in wartime and among civilians huddled in air raid shelters in the blitz. With Alcoholics Anonymous such public confession is rightly regarded as a therapy. Moral rearmament groups delighted to testify to past misdemeanors while, at a Pentecostal meeting recently, I listened to a young priest in Boston urged, apparently by the Spirit, to stand up and spout about his sins. Though such a performance seemed to me slightly artificial, I stuffed my handkerchief into my mouth to discourage the Holy Ghost.

It is not just the godly who like speaking about their sins for the ungodly are still more voluble. This may be seen at any bar among those who have had one too much. Alcohol makes many a man maudlin and he then weeps over his past wickedness. As one funny man said to me, "If you want us to make a good confession, why not place a bottle of Scotch at the head of the queue?"

Fooling apart, how much it helps us to share our guilt. I have met those who dislike confessing to a priest, who dislike the confessional, but it is rare indeed to meet someone who dislikes talking about past sins. How many, in our day, to gain such an opportunity, gladly pay a psychiatrist.

At this point allow me to introduce Dr. Paul Tournier, the distinguished Swiss psychiatrist. Dr. Tournier is a devout

Calvinist. He writes with deep understanding of the value of confessing our sins. In the first passage that I quote, he is answering the charge of some theologians that he is playing the part of the priest. He replies:

> I have often written about confession already but the misunderstanding still persists. The fear has been expressed by theologians that I am enlisting the doctor to take the place of the priest. I have not done so and never shall. That the Roman Catholic must seek sacramental absolution, that we must urge him to do so and that he cannot excuse himself on the pretext that he has confessed to his doctor—all this is clear: one cannot make one's peace with God by cheating one's church.
>
> But the theologians must see things as they really are and not as they would like them to be. There are around us vast numbers of people who are sick for confession, even among Roman Catholics and Eastern Christians, even among those who go regularly and sincerely to confession and who may suddenly, in a personal conversation, realise that they are guilty of wrongs that are of much more decisive importance for their lives than any they have so far confessed. Moreover there are those who have kept away from their church precisely to escape confession and who will be able to return to it as a result of a liberating hour spent with their doctor.
>
> And, then, there are the Protestants, among whom the practice of confession has fallen into grave disuse. Pastor Thurian has recently recalled with what clear insistence the reformers enjoined the regular practice of confession. Lastly there are the unbelievers, the half-believers, the agnostics and even those who are violently and aggressively anti-religious. They have as much need as believers of expressing their remorse.[3]

Here Dr. Tournier makes many a capital point. We do not go to confession because the Church tells us but because we need to for our fulfillment and happiness. I like his sentence "There are around us vast numbers of people who are sick for confession" for this exactly meets my own experience. Lack of confession may in time induce a deep spiritual sickness, the symptoms of which are widespread today. A devout Christian psychiatrist and a retreat director are both aware of this.

The old adage *Mens sana in corpore sano* contains more than a grain of truth. If a sound mind depends on a healthy body, so does a healthy body require a sound mind. The medical men of today, more fully accepting the power of mind over matter, publish lists of physical illnesses mentally induced. If we take just one further step backwards, it is easy to see the power of the spiritual over body and mind alike. A sick soul plays havoc with our mental balance and may cause ulcers and indigestion, too. A deep and enduring sense of guilt corrodes the toughest life. I have noticed over thirty years a rapid increase in tension and much of this in origin is spiritual. In the headlong flight from fear, loneliness, and failure, men fall back on drink and drugs or forward into deep depression and, with Hamlet, think about suicide. In a recent study of suicide, the estimate was given for countries who keep accurate records of a thousand suicides a day. Such figures cannot include the number of fatal accidents permitted by those who have no wish to live.

In the gospel story, the recurring link between sin and sickness is greatly emphasized. I grow more and more certain that such a connection is valid and should not be brushed aside.

Four hundred years ago, in Tudor London, Sir Thomas More, the man for all seasons, made this very point. He was competing with his children in their homework and, it would seem, dashed off an English essay on *The Four Last Things*. In his quaint and endearing English, he pointed out to his children the ravages caused by certain sins on the human face:

> Now let us see what help we may have of this medicine against the sickness of envy which is, undoubtedly, both a sore torment and a very consumption. For surely, envy is such a torment as all the tyrants in Sicily never devised a sorer. And it so drinks up the moisture of the body and consumes the good blood, so discolours the face, so defaces the beauty, so disfigures the visage, leaving it all bony, lean, pale and wan, that a person, well set-a-work with envy, needs no other image of death than his own face in a glass.[4]

The bottling up of such a spiritual sickness as envy may lead to nervous breakdowns and to melancholy. Four hundred years after Thomas More, Dr. Tournier, drawing on his clinical experience, makes the same point. He writes:

> I could give very many examples especially of patients who have come to visit me only once—often from a great distance—with the sole purpose of finding someone to whom they can confess a sin that has been weighing them down for years. They are often bewildering cases in which I have done nothing, practically said nothing: for which I have done no more than silently pray. Or, perhaps, I have by a few kind words helped them to make their confession more concrete. There remains nothing for me to do but remind them, in one way or another, that "If we confess our sins, he is faithful and righteous to forgive our sins and to cleanse us from all unrighteousness" (1 John 1:9). In many cases I have had neither time nor opportunity to make a medical examination or to prescribe a medicine and yet, a little while later, I have received a letter telling me that some morbid symptom that no medical treatment had been able to cure has disappeared, either at once or gradually.[5]

If Dr. Tournier is right, and my long experience as both a sinner and a confessor supports him, confession is a crying need today. How accurate his diagnosis that thousands around us are sick for confession and how sure his assertion that many tensions and morbid symptoms derive from this deficiency. Tournier is not alone among psychiatrists in this. William James writes feelingly about the value of confession, as does Dr. Viktor Frankl in his *The Doctor and the Soul*. How strange that while the psychiatrists stress the therapeutic value of confession and forgiveness, Christians, reared in the tradition of the sacrament, are dissatisfied.

The sacrament of penance is now out of favor, and a practice which we in childhood took very much for granted is now disregarded or spoken of with scorn. Far be it from me to condemn such Christians and their dissatisfaction for this in itself seems to point to something wrong. In recent years, in every retreat, at every question-and-answer session, queries about confession have pride of place. Let this be the justification for my book.

I find no case of a sinner in the gospel who approached Christ for forgiveness and went away sad. The Samaritan woman, with a tally of seven men, left Christ so excited that she had to tell the whole village of her relief. That shrewd little taxgatherer, Zacheus, whipped out his checkbook just as soon as he could scramble down from that sycamore tree. It was his suggestion that he should pay fourfold for past deceits. Christ paid no attention when Peter said, "Depart from me for I am a sinful man, O Lord."

2. Out of the depths

To appreciate the malice of sin and the joy of forgiveness, we need first to know ourselves. We are not flat fish. We have depths and three dimensions and live on three levels simultaneously. As the great Austrian psychiatrist Dr. Viktor Frankl puts it, "Man lives in three dimensions, the somatic, the mental, and the spiritual."[1] Just as a motorist takes his automatic gears for granted, so we move from one dimension to another without conscious thought. It pays, however, to know something of these three dimensions if we are to understand ourselves.

When I was young, man was presumed to have only two dimensions, and every good Christian child, well instructed, knew that man was made up of body and soul. Such a division is now outdated but by no means false. Just as gallons and pints will long survive the introduction of the metric system, so John Brown's body will lie a-moldering in the grave while his soul goes marching on.

The division of man into body and soul is useful but restrictive; it fails to tell the full story, it tends to provide an inaccurate picture of an unreal world. We come to regard our bodies as lumpish, lazy, and mulish and our souls as bright, ethereal, ghostly, something of will-o'-the-wisp. Nearly everyone presumes that the soul lives inside the body, when things may well be the other way round. After all, my memory may jump back fifty years in a second, while my body remains seated and gulping down a can of Diet Coke. Many a time, my heart communes with friends across the Atlantic without trying to take my body along. When his sister St. Scholastica died, St. Benedict saw her soul winging away towards heaven as a dove: while not for a moment doubting the great saint's vision, we might think that he was seeing a thing or two.

Advances in two very different fields of learning throw doubt on the competence of the body-soul approach. Scripture scholars point out that such a view was unknown in the early part of the Bible and that the great patriarchs saw man as a whole. The division of man into body and soul was Greek in origin and, with the rapid spread of Greek culture, worked its way into later Hebrew thought. But when Christ cried on the cross, "Father, into Thy hands I commend my spirit," may we say that he meant by spirit exactly what we mean by soul?

If modern Scripture scholars deserve our attention, so do modern psychologists. At the turn of the century psychology, as we now know it, was in its early infancy. Through half a century of astonishing growth, psychology has taught us to think of man as an individual person, with body and soul fusing to produce a whole. The apple tree in my garden achieves just this when roots, trunk, leaves, and sap work together, play their parts, and survive in the new fruit.

This theory which sounds so novel is, in fact, as old as the hills. Poets, philosophers, mystics, without using psychological jargon, have known about the three dimensions for centuries. As I hope to show later—this is a vital point in any approach to confession—Christ emphasized the three dimensions consistently. As for the rest, each poet, mystic, thinker has his or her individual way of describing our composition but the three dimensions of human consciousness stay the same. Dr. Frankl states categorically, "Man lives in three dimensions, the somatic, the mental, and the spiritual," to which an audience of experts, headed by St. Teresa of Ávila and St. Augustine, would certainly reply, "Hear! Hear!"

St. Teresa of Ávila is forever writing of the higher and lower parts of the soul. She is, also, an expert at mixing metaphors and has no sooner asked us to "turn to our castle with its many mansions" when she breaks off to exclaim, "Think of the palmito."[2] The point of the palmito, as she explains, is that it has many layers of outer rind which need removing before the savory center is exposed. St. Augustine discovered two wills in himself and after many years of effort came to identify the higher or deeper one with his heart.

From different viewpoints, the experts saw the three dimensions in different ways. For William James, there were the "Once Born" and the "Twice Born" and, in the center of our being, the "Red Hot Point" of consciousness. Freud recognized the Super-Ego, the Ego, and the Id. Dr. Sherwood Taylor preferred simple headings, our public life, our private life, and our inner life. In his *I'm OK–You're OK* Dr. Thomas Harris is highly original; each baby is born with a built-in tape recorder and three tapes, recording simultaneously.[3] Our *Parental* tape records the rules laid down by parents, priests, and teachers; the *Baby* tape gives our childish reactions; the *Adult* tape, by a process of selection, puts together our personal and mature point of view. For good measure, let me end this paragraph with Shakespeare, whose genius could present the three dimensions on the stage. So we see Hamlet, the young and popular prince of Denmark, talking to himself in secret, and choosing suicide.

If there are three dimensions in us all, we must see our lives in triplicate. There will be three kinds of prayer to fit our three dimensions, three kinds of silence, three ways of reading the Bible, three levels in making our confession, three types of sin. Part of the problem in the sacrament of penance has been the rolling of the three expressions of sin and sorrow into one.

Three seems to be the significant number, and yet no one has suggested that we are made up of three distinct persons on the pattern of the Holy Trinity. That there is a true reflection of the Godhead, I am certain, and no doubt we shall see the connection one day. At present we know ourselves to be each a single, individual person, living on three levels and showing three faces to those who know us best. Given a lampshade of three colors, the one bulb, viewed from different angles, may appear wholly blue, green, or red.

By far the most popular illustration of our makeup is taken from an actor on the stage. No theme in literature has proved more poignant than that of the clown, weary and brokenhearted, behind his grinning mask. As the experts tell us, the very word "person" derives from the masks used in Greek drama to disguise the face and to amplify the voice. Anyone who is able to grasp the difference between the person of the actor and the impersonation which he is performing comes very near to understanding the human mystery.

One point is now certain to me, that we all are actors; it is not a case of some being actors and others not. If men live "in three dimensions, the somatic, the mental, and the spiritual," then we may consider our powers of acting, on the somatic level first. Somatic means no more than the physical dimension in which our bodies strut upon the stage. In language, the active voice covers this operation in which we strive to reach the real physical world of people and to sell ourselves. Life on this level smacks of the footlights, for we are out to win an audience. We yearn to be noticed, to be heeded, to be applauded, to be loved. Dr. Sherwood Taylor used the label "Social Life" to describe our performance on life's stage. Over the years, such words as "society" and "social" have acquired a theatrical tang. At how many social gatherings we and others are busy acting, using a mask and giving an impersonation of ourselves.

It would be wrong to convey the impression that everyone in public is always artificial, always acting; nor is such acting always wrong. We were made that way and should recognize the fact. Yet it proves salutary from time to time and also amusing to look through our wardrobes, our jewel cases, and the cabinets in the bathroom jammed with toilet preparations to help us look our very best. Some among the moderns take equal trouble to make themselves always look their very worst. My act as a priest hardly requires your ties, cuff links, beards and mustaches for I must look holy at any cost. These are the trappings of actors and to them we add our wigs, medals, status symbols, and a script which includes name dropping, a witty sentence or two, and the very latest joke. I cease looking holy if another gets a laugh by telling my joke.

We may note in passing that religion also has a social level and a liturgy designed to be staged.

Shakespeare with "All the world's a stage" beautifully conveyed the lesson as, sixty years before him, did Sir Thomas More. More wrote:

> If you noticed that some silly actor was inordinately proud of wearing a golden coronet while taking the part of an Earl in a stage play, would you not laugh at his foolishness, knowing

> full well that when the play is finished, he must put on his own shabby clothes and walk home in them? But don't you yourself also feel very smart and proud to wear an actor's outfit, forgetting that when your part is completed, you too will walk off the stage as poor as he? Nor do you care to note that your play may end just as soon as his.[4]

The poor actor returns home in his shabby clothes. As he leaves the stage and audience behind him, he retires to that second dimension in which men may express themselves. Dr. Frankl labels this the mental dimension. Sherwood Taylor calls it our private life. In language, this dimension is often covered by the passive voice, for we are no longer actively engaged in reaching others but sit back and let the world pour into us. This second dimension has a charm about it for those who love reading, music, color, nature, solitude, and thought.

At first sight, the tranquillity of the second dimension is due to the absence of an audience. We do what we want when we are alone. In the physical dimension we behave ourselves, for the curtain has risen and we must give an impersonation of ourselves. Once alone with the door shut, our consciousness is centered on ourselves. We live inside our heads. We relax, let our hair down, put our feet up and our teeth in a glass. William James said as much to the audience in Edinburgh at the start of his famous Gifford lectures; he began, "All of you sit here with a certain constraint because of the influence of the occasion," and went on to describe how different it would be if each listener was alone.

When alone many make a beeline for the phone. Others study the mirror in the hope that they look younger or for fear that they have cancer of the tongue. One friend confessed that he wrote furious letters to the papers but had never posted one. Another shyly showed me his conductor's baton: "Yes," said he, "I switch on the radio every evening; I have longed to conduct an orchestra all my life."

Anthony Trollope's glorious description of Archdeacon Grantly in his study, for me, gets near to the bone:

> After breakfast, on the morning of which we are writing, the archdeacon, as usual, retired to his study intimating that he was going to be very busy, but that he would see Mr. Chadwick if he called. On entering this sacred room, he carefully opened the paper case on which he was wont to compose his favourite sermons, and spread on it a fair sheet of paper, and one partly written on; he then placed his inkstand, looked at his pen and folded his blotting paper; having done so, he got up again from his seat, stood with his back to the fire-place and yawned comfortably, stretching out vastly his huge arms and opening his burly chest. He then walked across the room and locked the door; and having so prepared himself, he threw himself into his easy chair, took from a secret drawer beneath his table a volume of Rabelais, and began to amuse himself with the witty mischief of Panurge; and so passed the archdeacon's morning on that day.[5]

Watching Archdeacon Grantly, we may ask ourselves the question, are we entirely free of acting and self-impersonation when we are alone? The very existence of reflexive verbs in the structure of every language brings out the duplicity which is ours. Such common expressions as "George fairly gave himself away," "She was beside herself with anger," "I like my own company" all suggest that two people, not one, inhabit our minds and our rooms. One of the more frightening of such expressions, "Pull yourself together," implies the constant fear that we may lose our self-control. The very phrase "self-control" postulates a second person, another me in the driving seat. To soliloquize is to talk to yourself, and in this lies the genius of Shakespeare, for he could expose the duplicity of our second dimension on a first dimensional stage.

Few writers have better understood the problems of our second dimension than the great American psychologist William James. Of New England, Presbyterian stock—he once thought of joining the ministry—James suffered a nervous breakdown after completing his studies at the Harvard Medical School. Recovering completely from this dark night of the soul, he gave his life to the study of the causes of such mental and spiritual distress. He, who began so uncertainly, finished as one of the most tranquil and balanced personalities of his day. James was the first American to be invited to lecture in a European university and he chose for his Gifford lectures in Edinburgh "The Varieties of Religious Experience."

These lectures were published in a book which became a classic, one of the most helpful books that I have ever read. James did not invent the titles "Once-Born" and "Twice-Born" but he believed in the distinction and made it his own. So he opened his study of religion with an amusing lecture on the "Healthy-Minded," those simple, extrovert types who know no problem that cannot be cured by a dose of salts and a good stiff walk. Next, he introduces the "Twice-Born," introvert and full of doubts. For these much perplexity lies ahead. The naïve faith and practice of their childhood has to wither if they are to be born psychologically again. Undoubtedly James had suffered this himself. He illustrates the process in the stories of such great men as Luther, Tolstoy, Bunyan, Wesley, Robert Louis Stevenson. Many of his sources, because of his own background, are Protestant. He himself belonged to no denomination, was well read in Catholic faith and practice, critical of certain saints who seemed to him narrow and stunted, in particular of St. Aloysius, St. Margaret Mary, and St. John of the Cross. He wrote warmly of the value of the Catholic confessional, and saw it as a great aid for the healthy-minded, who could thus shed their worries, clean the slate and start again.

I found James helpful especially in his eighth lecture on "The Divided Self." He took for granted as part of our psychological evolution the neurotic tensions which trouble many of us. The solution lies in accepting our makeup with its built-in duplicity. Life in this second dimension may prove full and rewarding but it may also bring acute distress. Drink, drugs, inferiority complexes, scruples, bouts of depression pertain to this dimension as, of course, do thoughts about suicide. Even when I am off stage and back in the greenroom, I still impersonate myself to myself.

Deeply religious people learn to accept the reality of a third dimension, the shadow of which is seen in our duplicity. For this reason Teresa of Ávila wrote of the higher part of the soul and the lower, and Thomas More knew a secret room within him, "the secret chamber of the mind, the privy-closet of the soul." Augustine tells us, "I carried my soul as if it were sliced in sunder and gored with blood and impatient even to be carried by me." Indeed, Augustine in his *Confessions* shows himself a master of this personal analysis and psychology. The duplicity inside himself both alarmed and tickled him. He was baffled to discover that a man may disobey himself. After a shrewd remark, "Ordinarily, indeed, a man does not laugh alone," he goes on to describe laughter on a lower level, when he had tricked his friends. "It was a delight and laughter which tickled us even to the very heart to think that we were deceiving those who feared no such thing of us."

Perhaps the most vivid account of the discovery of the

third dimension was written by Alphonse Daudet and is quoted by William James:

> Homo Duplex; Homo Duplex. The first time that I perceived that I was two was at the death of my brother Henri, when my father cried out so dramatically, "He is dead, he is dead." While my first self wept, my second self thought, "How truly given was that cry, how fine it would be at the theatre." I was then fourteen years old.
>
> This horrible duality has often given me matter for reflection. Oh, this terrible second me, always seated while the other is on foot, acting, living, suffering, bestirring itself. This second me that I have never been able to intoxicate, to make shed tears or to put to sleep. And how it sees into things and how it mocks.[6]

Here Alphonse Daudet hits the nail squarely on the head. Such secret dissatisfaction with themselves, with their duplicity, corrodes many seemingly successful lives. The girl who has married well, the priest who is well received, the businessman who has done very well on the social level are, all too often, painfully ashamed of themselves. I myself have been astonished over the years at the number of those who socially love to brag about their successes, their humor, their many talents, but who in secret hate themselves. On his forty-fourth birthday, in his private diary, Evelyn Waugh touched on the three dimensions, but with no joy: "Guilt is beginning as my memory goes feeble. I am a very much older man than this time last year, physically infirm and lethargic. Mentally I have reached a stage of non-attachment which if combined with a high state of prayer (as it is not) would be edifying. I have kept none of the resolutions made this day, a year ago. I have vast reasons for gratitude and am seldom conscious of them."

For so many of us this innate duplicity wears us down. We sweep the dust under the mat, lock the skeleton in the cupboard, drink and try to hide the bottles, dodge every medical checkup, postpone, put off, compromise, cover up but with no hope of escape. We cry out with Daudet, "Oh, this terrible second me," not fully grasping that this second me is our very person, yearning to break through the tissue of subterfuge.

The acceptance of dual personality and the effort to recognize and respect the second me, who is always mocking, in the end brings peace and stability. The merit of William James lies in his willingness to admit that the divided self is a normal stage in development. Dr. Jung thought the same. In the book written shortly before his death, Jung discussed this seeming division in himself: "The play and counterplay between Personalities One and Two, which has run throughout my life, has nothing to do with 'split' or dissociation in the ordinary medical term. On the contrary, it is played out in every individual." So we are not mad or schizophrenic and once we face this division into two personalities, our problems are through. The wider the division between personalities One and Two, the greater our sanity, the sharper our humor, for each personality gains more room for maneuver, may stand back further to see and to laugh at the other self.

Augustine solved his problem when he accepted the third dimension and, of a sudden, found there his true self. What he found in fact was his own free will. He said to God, and I modernize the English, "What drew me to your light was the recognition that I had a will of my own and of this I am as certain as that I am alive. When I chose anything or did not choose it, I knew for certain that it was I myself and no one else who made the choice; and I saw that in this lay the cause and root of my sin."[7]

So we come to the heart of the matter, the third dimension

which so many philosophers, psychiatrists, poets, saints, mystics have tried to explain. For William James as, I think, for Fr. Teilhard de Chardin, our true Ego lives at the red-hot point of consciousness. Freud is also concerned with consciousness as an escape from repression and his will-to-pleasure principle examines the roots of sex. Dr. Frankl finds in the center of the heart a will-to-meaning; Dr. Tournier focuses on the person lying behind all the layers of impersonation, by which we give an imitation of the kind of person we think we ought to be.

We all are different in this third, spiritual dimension, for each human person is unique. I have derived the greatest help about our inner life not from William James, St. Teresa, Teilhard de Chardin but from a man who professed chemistry and who published several chemistry and general science textbooks for schools. Only at the end of his life did Dr. F. Sherwood Taylor write a book about religion, a slight volume of a hundred pages entitled *Two Ways of Life.* Other writers are neat, as was St. Teresa with her *Interior Castle,* or poetic as is Teilhard de Chardin, or academic with William James. Sherwood Taylor hits off exactly the delicacy, vagueness, and confusion at the very center of our hearts. Here is an uncharted region, swathed with clouds. When we think of examining our conscience, confessing sins, expressing sorrow, we need to make allowance for these clouds.

Dr. Sherwood Taylor's description has greatly helped me since 1947 when I read it first. I quoted it in an earlier book. Without apology I again repeat it to bring this complicated chapter to its close:

> This inner life is lived in a strange enough world; for in truth each man and woman dwells in a different environment—so dif-

ferent that I believe that there are no two people who have so much as half in common. Men know each other's inner world so slightly that they neglect this difference and it is only when two people have a relation of utter love and trust that their inner lives begin to be perceptible to each other and are revealed as mutually most strange.

What are the constituents of this inner life? First there are memories of men and places and actions, a few pages curiously selected from countless volumes of experience—curiously selected and strangely distorted, as we find when old memories are confronted with the things remembered. There is a system, or at least a view of the world, constructed from principles whose origin is the thoughts and conclusions of ourselves and of others; whether known in the flesh or through their writings; some of these principles being casual and ill grasped sojourners, others smoothed and hardened by constant use into habits of thought and action. Memories and thoughts may be records of fact, or symbols of something within ourselves, or both of these; and always in the depth of the mind an unknown agent fashions for us symbols, fantasies and images which are manifest in dreams but also well up into and tinge the rational thoughts of our waking hours. All these are as it were the matter of the mind; but there are forces also—loves and hates, the magnetic drawing of the mind to beauty, truth, goodness, of the body to the objects of its desire. Above, within, beyond all these, we know the controlling I, who knows them, who knows that I can within ill-defined and uncertain limits choose what I shall think and what I shall do; Plato's charioteer driving his ill-matched team.

Perhaps deeper, or perhaps less clearly apprehended, are certain knowings which are not facts or yet desires, the knowing and turning to something that is changeless, that is not seen or heard by sense or imagination; something that remains when the tumult of the mind is hushed, when even the I is still and waiting. In this region there are no words, no images, but there is

> that to which every thought and fantasy and imagining and desire are subject.[8]

This may not describe your third dimension but it exactly covers mine and sets out the various layers of the third dimension unerringly. Let me set out the headings thus:

1 Curiously selected memories, often inaccurate.
2 A view of the world based on memories, conversations, books.
3 Habits of thought and action.
4 Dreams and fantasies which color rational thought.
5 The magnetic attraction of the mind to beauty, truth, goodness.
6 Of the body to the objects of its desire.
7 The capital "I," aware of its mastery and responsibility.
8 The yearning towards the changeless; not imaginable.
9 Absolute quiet in the awareness of that to which all thought is subject.

Religion and confession begin with points eight and nine of this catalogue. All the accounts of great conversions veer towards these two points. Dr. Tournier adds a third:

> There is, also, an irresistible force within, which compels us to be honest to the bitter end, to throw off the mask of personage and uncover the person. When my patient is in the throes of this struggle, his almost inaudible words are broken by long silences; there is taking place within him another inner dialogue. This second dialogue is with God, even if the man concerned is not a believer and thinks he is only wrestling with himself. His whole being resists as we all do; if he speaks it no longer comes from himself but from a force more powerful than he. The woman I mentioned who said "You are implacable" was simply uttering aloud an answer from her inner dialogue.[9]

When we speak of sin, sorrow, confession, a firm purpose of amendment, we are telling the truth but in unreal, academic terms. Posturing on the human stage, or worrying ourselves as actors in the greenroom we are still impersonating and playing a part. Only in the third dimension can we clowns get rid of our masks.

3. Jesus Christ, psychiatrist

No flippancy is intended when I call Christ a psychiatrist. The title is relevant today, exactly fits the gospel story and emphasizes the delicacy of that sacrament by which our sins are washed away.

Many other titles have been given to Christ: "Christ the King," "Jesus the Messiah," "Light of the World," "God Incarnate," but these have their roots in Scripture and theology. Thousands today, following in the footsteps of Nathanael and Nicodemus, are drawn to Christ through his authority. There are, however, thousands of others who remain unbelievers and yet are conscious of Christ's magnetic power. The title "Christ the Psychiatrist" preserves the reactions of those sick and sinful people in the gospel who knew nothing of other titles but were attracted by his understanding and sympathy. That little old lady who had suffered hemorrhage for years perhaps knew nothing of Jesus the Messiah but felt compelled to touch him in her misery.

In the sphere of psychology, Christ was some twenty centuries ahead of his day. His uncanny appreciation of human beings and their motivation gave him his mastery. Truths which he tossed off in a casual sentence would later be discovered by the experts and expanded into impressive tomes. For all our modern advances in psychotherapy, I sometimes wonder if we know as much about life's real problems as did those simple people listening to Christ in Galilee.

William James helps to illustrate this point with his collection of cases which record the varieties of religious experience. Perhaps two thirds of these hinge on a changing relationship with Jesus Christ. Centuries after his death, at the deepest level, he could bring peace and purpose to clever but unhappy men. What strange bedfellows were these? We find Luther and Augustine, Tolstoy and Wesley rubbing shoulders with that freethinking French Jew, M. Alphonse Ratisbonne. To synopsize Ratisbonne's account, he remarked in effect, later, "If anyone had said to me, 'Alphonse, in a quarter of an hour, you'll be adoring Jesus Christ as your God and Saviour,' I would have judged him mad."

The Christian mystics afford us a further illustration for, to judge from their spiritual writings, no two of them were anything like the same. To each his or her special vision, in that third dimension to which Christ so frequently referred. Deep in that misty world where resides the capital "I", each had a unique and personal experience and exchanged personal love. In the third dimension, all generalizations are invalid except one. The mystics had one common factor, a personal relationship with Christ. Otherwise, they differed greatly in style, emotion, imagination, environment, and thought. Thus St. Teresa of Ávila and St. John of the Cross were contemporaries and intimate friends, laboring in the same country and in the same religious order for the same reforms. Yet their contemplative lives, to judge by what they wrote, were entirely different. I once read in a learned journal how, when Teresa and John were in Toledo, Teresa, who had much trouble with prickly confessors, never thought of approaching her friend and fellow Doctor of the Church. Yet Teresa and John of the Cross are invariably grouped together; imagine the gap between this Spanish pair and Augustine, Bernard, De Caussade, Evelyn Underhill, Simone Weil, and Dag Hammarskjöld. In the third dimension, Christ fashioned a relationship with each individual through a person-to-person approach. Dr. Frankl, Dr. Tournier, and other great psychiatrists would agree that this is the only approach.

To appreciate Christ's technique and all that he added to man's yearning for forgiveness, it helps to consider what happened before his day. Man was there, sin was there, and guilt was there, all the world over, and in the most primitive forms of tribal worship there were penitential purifying rites. Sin in this primitive state was not personal but little more than an amalgam of magic and taboos. In much the same way as bad luck is predicted today for a man who is hardy enough to walk under a ladder, so in primitive days an arbitrary good or bad luck decided man's fate. He was a digit and could do nothing but seek outside help. So he invoked magic, and his confessor was the magician or the medicine man. We meet such magic in the Acts of the Apostles and vague traces of a primitive mentality survive in some Christian churches in our day.

The more sophisticated societies gradually freed themselves from the bonds of magic, and sin for these became the infringement of a code. Where more primitive people purged their sins in the first dimension by ritual washings, the philosophers retired to the second dimension with right reason as their guide. Sin was an offense against reason and the sinner could only kick himself for behaving like a fool. Here was the philosophy of doing the right thing, behaving sensibly, with all the discipline and self-denial which these demand. How greatly one must admire men of the caliber of Cicero, Seneca, the Emperor Marcus Aurelius, along with their counterparts today. But a moral code based on reason alone differs little from the code of conduct taught by Victorian nannies and praised on Prize Days by earnest headmasters in Victorian public schools. It proves insufficient in the face of misery and guilt to say, "I could kick myself, I have behaved badly, I have let the side down, I am a something fool." Yet this mentality is still met among Christian people for whom the confessional box is a spiritual police court or a psychiatrist's consulting room.

When we turn to the Old Testament, we discover a far deeper appreciation of sin. We now have a personal God, loving and paternal, in so many respects a patriarch. He made the laws as in the garden of Eden, gave rewards and punishments. With the Old Testament, love and sorrow entered religion; King David lay on the ground weeping, where no tears of sorrow were shed by Cicero. Yet despite such moving accounts of sorrow and forgiveness, sin for the bulk of the Hebrew people was a national, tribal transgression of the law. The whole race had signed a covenant with God. Moses was forever asking the people to be faithful, and the high priest on the day of atonement prayed as spokesman for the people, "O God, I have committed iniquity, transgressed and sinned before thee, I and my house."

Some elements of these three attitudes to sin and sorrow have survived. For some magic, in the form of superstition, plays a part in the sacrament of penance, for others sin, as a breach of the moral code, is shameful while, for most Christians, a true sense of infidelity has been borrowed from Old Testament times. The whole approach to sin alters with the coming of Jesus Christ. Yet Christ was emphatic that he had not come to abolish the law of Moses but to fulfill it, and we may ask ourselves how did he set about achieving this? He did not amend the Mosaic law, as we may amend a constitution, nor did he tamper with ancient Hebrew liturgy. I would suggest that he fulfilled the law and brought it to life through his profound psychological insight of human needs. It may well be that such a revolutionary change demanded incarnation, for the person-to-person approach requires, at least in the beginning, a human being whom all can touch and hear and see.

To drive the point home, allow me to quote once more those lines by Dr. Sherwood Taylor which delineate the region in which Christ would work:

> This inner life is lived in a strange enough world; for in truth each man and each woman dwells in a different environment—so different that I believe that no two people have so much as half in common. Men know each other's inward world so slightly that they neglect the difference and it is only when two people have a relationship of utter love and trust that their inner lives begin to become perceptible to each other and are revealed as mutually most strange.

Such a barrier between persons is a commonplace of life and few manage to scale it; in the gospel story any such barrier is thrown up only by the sinner, never by Christ.

The first striking feature of Christ's method is his influence with the individual person, rarely with a crowd. He drew multitudes but somehow failed to hold them and he had only a handful of faithful friends around him when he died. The crowds wanted to make him king for the wrong reasons; they followed him only for signs and wonders and, to use his own expression, "were dull of heart." Even the enthusiasm generated on Palm Sunday could not last five days. I see a mystery here. Where the Holy Spirit after Pentecost inspired mass conversions, Christ never did. As John reports at the start of Christ's crusade, "While he was in Jerusalem for the feast, there were many who came to believe in his name seeing the miracles that he did. But Jesus would not give them his confidence; he had knowledge of them all and did not need assurances about any man because he could read men's hearts."[1]

What was so unusual about Christ's method? I would say his third dimensional approach. For him it was the person, not the various impersonations, which counted most. He knew all about the divided self, the sick soul, man's search for meaning, the very subjects about which our modern psychiatrists write. Christ reached the clown behind the mask. Surely it was this sympathy and understanding that gave him so many personal relationships. He treated each individual differently. Thus he appreciated the fear of the Pharisee Nicodemus, frightened for his reputation, and hence calling on Jesus after dark. This to Christ was genuine, not play-acting like the hospitality of Simon, another Pharisee. Simon's impersonation was brushed aside, but the tears of the prostitute who gate-crashed the party were accepted as sincere. At the very moment when Pontius Pilate was preparing to condemn him, Christ informed this well-intentioned pagan that his was the lesser sin. Peter had publicly denied his master; it took one glance, not to deflate but to forgive him, with the relief of bitter tears.

In one of the most pithy of his parables about sin, Christ showed how little he was fooled by play-acting, how greatly he loved those who were sincere. The Pharisees had been murmuring about the company he kept and Christ threw up a question, his frequent and favorite technique:

> "Tell me what you think; there was a man who had two sons and when he went up to the first and said, 'Away with thee, my son and work in my vineyard today,' he answered, 'Not I,' but he relented afterwards and went. Then he went up to the

other and said the like to him and his answer was 'I will, Sir' but he did not go. Which of these two carried out his father's will?" "The first," they said. And Jesus said to them, "Believe me, the publicans and harlots are further on the road to God's kingdom than you."

I love this parable for the boy who said "No" on his first and second dimensions said "Yes" in his heart.

I am unable to think of any other philosopher, statesman, religious leader who based every judgment on one virtue only, sincerity. In the gospel, nothing is made of looks, wealth, intellectual talents, past reputations, good or bad. The original twelve certainly were unreliable, boastful, intolerant, doubting; one proved insincere. Peter was cowardly on one fatal occasion and a curious hesitancy continued throughout his life. St. Paul rebuked him for it and in the old, old story of *Quo Vadis?* Christ confronted a Peter running away from martyrdom. Yet Peter was offered a different chance and took it by the lakeside: when Christ asked him three times, "Simon, son of John, do you love me?" the apostle worded the most sincere prayer ever expressed. "Peter was upset that he asked him a third time, 'Do you love me?' and said, 'Lord, you know everything; you know I love you,'" invoking Christ's own knowledge as his proof. Had he said these words, "You know I love Christ," to James or John they might well have hesitated; they might have said, "You denied that you knew him only this day last week." Because Christ knew all Peter's weaknesses, he also knew the truth.

Dr. Tournier quotes a penetrating statement by a French doctor: "A complete confession is always necessary in medicine." The same is certainly true with Christ. And the answer to Addison's gibe that the act of contrition of a hypocrite is itself hypocritical is surely to be found in Peter's prayer.

Christ's preoccupation with sincerity is underlined in all his dealings with the Pharisees. Not all the Pharisees were bad. Many later became disciples and three were noble, Nicodemus, Gamaliel, and the "Pharisee of Pharisees," the great St. Paul. The fault of the Pharisees was to center their lives in the wrong dimension and to seek the applause of men. Christ himself, so severe in his criticism of their behavior, never denied their righteousness. He told his disciples, "Let your righteousness exceed the righteousness of the scribes and Pharisees," to which John Wesley added a shrewd rider, "Before we inquire how our righteousness may exceed theirs, let us examine whether at present we come up to it."

Consider the Pharisee who was praying in the temple, externally on every count a good man. He lived chastely, never cheated his neighbor, gave alms generously, and fasted twice a week. Had the temple had its confessional box, he would have been scratching his head and puzzling what to confess. But I suspect that he would have made a confession frequently to edify others and to create a good effect. His one mistake was a common one of living in the first dimension and acting his faith on the stage. He was, in fact, an actor giving a brilliant impersonation of a holy man. Actors and actresses often remark how they perform better if they believe in the part that they are asked to play. Our Pharisee believed in his part, he loved the law, the liturgy, Sabbath day observance, was proud of his vocation and welcomed the self-discipline which it entailed. His only fault was the desire to be clapped. The Pharisees, as Christ told the people, prayed to be seen praying, fasted to look austere, gave alms in public to get their names on to every worthwhile subscription list.

Christ asked of his disciples the opposite. They were to pray in secret, to disguise their fasting, to give alms in private so that they could burrow downwards to the third dimension to become and to be themselves. On these precise points, how many of us take Christ's injunctions seriously? If we do not, then we too are phony and our prayer is one that thanks God that we are not hypocrites like this Pharisee. I feel for that poor Pharisee. I remember the days when we young priests were urged to be edifying, to be seen praying by our congregations, to live austerely at least when any of the laity were round about. How many devout Christian parents put on an act to edify the children or the priest.

I know nothing about you, but I myself cannot recall a moment in my life when I could not say with St. Peter, "Lord, you know everything, you know I love you," but with a condition attached. When I examine that word "everything" and break it down, then my prayer takes on a sincere but side-splitting contradiction. "Lord, because you know my hypocrisies, you know I love you" is about the most honest prayer that man can voice.

When the elders complained that Christ's disciples ate food without a ritual washing, he answered with words from Isaiah, "This people honors me with their lips but their heart is far from me." Here, the third dimension is divided from the others and here, too, we meet Christ's deep psychological use of the word "heart."

In very form of language, the heart has been used to pinpoint the center of our being and it has been honored as the seat of all emotions, more especially of love. For a great many people today the heart has become the symbol for physical love, for sex, for that sensuous, sentimental emotion about which we hear in every second pop song, and at which we gaze yearly as St. Valentine's feast comes round. For some unexplained reason, the heart covers a boy and girl who are dating but not a young mother fondling her baby, who must make do with a diaper instead.

A similar maudlin use of the heart is found in religious language and devotional art. Christ himself was the victim of such emotionalism in certain epochs, especially in connection with the seventeenth-century devotion to the Sacred Heart. An understanding of Christ's use of the word "heart," an appreciation of his psychotherapy, might have spared us much embarrassment and the imagery of Guido Reni and Holman Hunt. A beautiful picture may also be untrue to life. I find nowhere in the gospel, or in St. Paul, any justification of that sentimentality which, in my boyhood, passed for piety. When Christ used the word "heart" he was always down to earth and, like any good doctor, both gentle and tough.

He used the word "heart" often, but always to indicate the third, spiritual dimension, incoherent, swathed in mist. Language itself gives to the word a profound, psychological meaning which may be expressed as "the real person" or "the real me." We speak of the purehearted, hardhearted, brokenhearted and Christ did the same. Thus the Pharisee who went to the temple "made this prayer in his heart, 'I thank thee God that I am not as other men.'" There was no acting, no impersonation, but a genuine, deep-seated superiority complex in this prayer. Again, Christ said of the Pharisees, "They have set their hearts on high places," and to them, "Why do you murmur in your hearts?" The same man who said, "A man who lusts after a woman in his heart has already committed adultery," remarked to the bystanders, "Learn of me for I am meek and humble of heart."

When you think of it, the heart may be good, bad, or indifferent but it is always genuine. In a heart-to-heart talk both parties mean what they say. If we say that Fred is eating his heart out, we mean that his frustrations, desires, heartaches are driving him to despair. To be of good heart implies a deep determination, to lose heart is to throw up everything. Finally we reach the heart of the matter and Jesus Christ, psychiatrist.

With the utmost sympathy and understanding, Christ peels away all layers of sham. First, with unusual emphasis, he stated categorically that evil does not come to us from outside. The audience was sufficiently puzzled for Christ to repeat the statement three times. After so many centuries of magic and taboos, the outward observance of rules and regulations, men could not grasp that they generate good and evil within themselves.

The scene is an impressive one, for Christ first turned on the Pharisees who had been secretly grumbling because the disciples had broken with tradition and eaten without first washing their hands. Christ in answer quoted Isaiah about lip service and made it clear that no food, washed or unwashed, is able to defile a man.

Next, he turned to the people, exclaiming, "Hear me all of you and understand; there is nothing outside a man which by going into him can defile him; but the things that come out of man are what defile him." Thus, at a stroke, he broke the tyranny of tradition and taboos.

Leaving the crowd and entering a house, he found the disciples puzzled and anxious to question him. "And he said to them, 'Then you are also without understanding? Do you not see, whatever goes into a man from outside cannot defile him since it enters not his heart but his stomach and so passes on? For, within, out of the heart of man come evil thoughts, fornication, theft, murder, adultery, deceit, licentiousness, envy, slander, pride, foolishness. All these evil things come from within and they defile a man.'"

Let me quote again, "A complete confession is always necessary in medicine," for this was the point towards which Christ had to work. He is scotching forever those two deceits mentioned by C. S. Lewis which enable us to kid ourselves indefinitely with "My heart is in the right place" and "I would not hurt a fly." Sooner or later we are driven back into a corner, we are forced to admit that, at the very center of our being, we are schemers, capable of every kind of underhand method to get what we want. Christ put this in one neat sentence, "Where your treasure is, there will your heart be too."

Christ knew men so well and loved them so much and treated each with so much sympathy and understanding that he drew from the sinners in the gospel that genuine confession which alone could bring them happiness. No force, physical or moral, was ever used. Christ never asked anyone to confess. He infused such confidence through his kindness that sinners came to him. His friends in the gospel had one mark in common, not innocence, not righteousness but spontaneous, homemade sincerity.

Christ returned to the theme of the heart on many occasions, not to find fault, to threaten, or to bluster but to teach men to know and to help themselves. Perhaps the most subtle of his psychological lessons turns on a fruit tree and its fruit. He said, "No good tree bears bad fruit nor again does a bad tree bear good fruit. Each tree is known by its fruit . . . The good man out of the good treasure of his heart produces good, and the evil man out of his evil treasure produces evil; for out of the abundance of the heart, the mouth speaks."

I remarked earlier how Christ would toss off a casual sentence which centuries later the experts would expand into tomes. This phrase "out of the abundance of the heart, the mouth speaks" may serve as an example for it forms the substance of many psychology books today. Christ's famous dictum is variously translated and we may take our pick. The more traditional renderings tell us that it is from the fullness, the abundance, the overflow of the heart that the mouth speaks. The Jerusalem Bible turns it the other way round:

"For a man's words flow out of what fills his heart." As a onetime schoolmaster I wince at one translation only; no boy in my class would have written "A man's mouth speaks what his heart is full of" and got away with it.

Whatever the translation, Christ's thought is clear. Good and evil are brewed in the third dimension and work their way outwards in thoughts and words and deeds. From the heart, my true desires, good or bad, will overflow into the other dimensions to affect not just thoughts and words but my voice, reading, haberdashery, friends, tastes, jokes. The very impersonations which I stage on the other levels are programed in the heart.

Dr. Viktor Frankl, in *The Doctor and the Soul,* sums up the theories about human motivation put forward by modern psychiatrists:

> Psychoanalysis speaks of the *pleasure principle,* individual psychology of the *status drive.* The pleasure principle might be termed the *Will-to-pleasure;* the status drive is equivalent to the *Will-to-power.* But where do we hear of that which most deeply concerns man; where is the innate desire to give as much meaning as possible to one's life, to actualize as many values as possible—what I should like to call the *Will-to-meaning?* This *Will-to-meaning* is the most human phenomenon of all since an animal certainly never worries about the meaning of its existence. Yet psychotherapy would turn this *Will-to-meaning* into a human frailty, a neurotic complex. A therapist who ignores man's spiritual side and who is thus forced to ignore the *Will-to-meaning* is giving away one of his most valuable assets. For it is to this will that a psychotherapist should appeal. Again and again we have seen that an appeal to continue life, to survive the most unfavorable conditions can be made only when such a survival appears to have a meaning. That meaning must be specific and personal, a meaning which can be realized by this

> one person alone. For we must never forget that every man is unique in the universe.[2]

Now Dr. Frankl is one of the leading international psychiatrists and when he asks, "Where do we hear of that which most deeply inspires man?" and fails to find an answer in his own profession, he should turn to the gospel for relief. Christ, in a passage already quoted, listed the evils which flow from the heart of man. Deep in the third dimension, you do not find this specific sin or that one but the will-to-pleasure which will overflow into the other dimensions as fornication, adultery, licentiousness. Nor do you find in the heart any specific sin of greed but the will-to-power which will be manufactured into slander, envy, pride, murder, theft. But what of the will-to-meaning? This too is fully illustrated in the gospel in the case of those poor sinners who were drawn to Christ. He put meaning into their lives—the aim of Dr. Frankl also—for which reason I call my chapter "Jesus Christ, psychiatrist."

4. Thank you, Eve

In a book about confession, dare one omit all reference to Adam and Eve? They started it. This endearing pair, so easily identified by their very lack of clothing, have been with us since our tenderest years. In childhood we were told about them and could see them being driven from the garden in our picture books. We were probably too young to appreciate that, when they first donned clothing, they began both man's first impersonation and first coverup.

There is no way of escaping from Adam and Eve. Visit any art gallery and there they will be, looking slightly sheepish; go to a night club and you should hear a joke about them, listen to a sermon and, sooner or later, the preacher will round on the hapless pair. Women may forget Eve but we men cannot get rid of Adam; we carry a chunk of his apple in our throats.

The story of Adam and Eve is, surely, one of the greatest ever told. It does not lose its magic because some progressive people label it a myth. A few of the details about the garden of Eden come under fire from botanists, paleontologists, geographers, and Women's Lib. Not a few Christians, on the defensive, feel that the story may be accepted only as legend or allegory. Such labels as allegory, legend, myth turn the tale of Adam and Eve into a fairy story, not to be taken too seriously.

Frankly, the use of such labels in no way destroys the truth of the story for me; allegory, poetry, history, myth are legitimate forms of revelation with the will-to-meaning as our goal. A historian myself, by taste and training, I find more truth in *Hamlet, Animal Farm,* or *Don Quixote* than in Lord Macauley's or Winston Churchill's history books. Why doubt the veracity of Genesis? Here we have one of the oldest stories in the world, recorded in detail by primitive people with a depth and subtlety rarely if ever achieved since. Further, without the fall of Adam and Eve we are doomed to live without meaning; lastly, it just so happens that we may check the truth of the story for ourselves.

We all know, by direct experience in our third dimension, that we have a fatal flaw within ourselves. When I say or think to myself, "Hang it all, I'm only human," I am using Adam and Eve as my excuse. Is there anyone who would not admit in his search for meaning that there are endless situations in which he dare not trust himself? Many of these are trivial. After a family squabble about washing-up, a teenage boy shouted hysterically to his mother, "You are acting like a typical teenager," and, as she added in a letter to me, "I certainly was." A dear old priest, long dead, used to put it sweetly, mumbling, "Lord, why did you make me such a bloody fool?" under what he thought, mistakenly, was his breath. The acceptance of such a flaw in ourselves becomes easier as we grow older, for the memory of past scenes, deceits, humiliations teaches us to tolerate ourselves.

No modern book helps more to link Adam's sin to our own search for meaning than William Golding's *Lord of the Flies.* Others must have found the same, for this best seller went through thirteen reprints in thirteen years. A review in the

London *Times* hit off exactly the moral of this devastating story, the spiritual collapse of those well-intentioned, nicely mannered, intelligent children, cut off without adult supervision, on a desert isle. Having taught boys of that very age, I could see my own little darlings behaving in the exact way that the author described. The review in the *Times* opens: "Mr. Golding knows exactly what boys are like; he has a compelling imagination and the vivid realism with which he describes the disintegration of their untried and precarious civilisation under the pressure of raw nature carries the reader to the bloody climax; a most absorbing and instructive tale."

Whether or not we label *Lord of the Flies* as myth or fable, it is exactly true to life. When those decent, innocent boys were left on their own, the will-to-pleasure and the will-to-power prevailed. When these led the pack to cruelty, greed, lust, fear, guilt, superstition, the only two boys who retained a will-to-meaning broke down in despair:

> Piggy took off his glasses, plainly troubled, "I dunno Ralph," he said, "We just got to go on, that's all. That's what the grown-ups would do . . . What makes things break up as they do?"[1]

Poor cross-eyed Piggy, blind without his glasses, was the one hero in the story; as anyone would guess who thinks of Good Friday, he paid for his honesty with his life. When the navy had arrived and the ragamuffins had come slinking from the woods to safety, the officer in charge saw Ralph. "In the middle of them, with filthy body, matted hair and unwiped nose, Ralph wept for the end of innocence, the darkness of man's heart and the fall through the air of the true, wise friend called Piggy."

The flaw in man, here played out by boys to the shame of Ralph and Piggy, has led many intelligent men and women to despair of the human race. As Thomas Hobbs put it, "The life of man is solitary, poor, nasty, brutish and short." Readers of my age have lived through two world wars and the slaughter of twenty million people; the exact figure is anybody's guess. Wars, sadism, lust, greed, money-grabbing induce in many a cynicism which burrows to our very roots. In answer to Piggy's query, "What makes things break up as they do?" we would all say: the selfishness of man. And the kernel of such an answer would carry us back to the Pharisee praying in the temple, "I thank thee, Lord, that I am not as other men."

A surprisingly large number of people today, each modestly admitting that he or she is different, would accuse mankind of letting the world down. Dear little old ladies feeding the birds, devoted housewives queuing for pet foods in the supermarket, ecologists with fanatical fire in their eyes, nature lovers, may well prefer animals to men. Once, at a private meeting which started in a friendly fashion, I was astonished to discover that thirteen people out of sixteen thought that animals were better than men. Walt Whitman in a celebrated passage expressed such an attitude well:

> I could turn and live with animals, they are so placid and self-contained.
> I stand and look at them, long and long.
> They do not sweat and whine about their condition.
> They do not lie awake in the dark and weep for their sins.
> Not one is dissatisfied, not one is demented with the mania for owning things.
> Not one kneels to another, nor to his kind that lived thousands of years ago.
> Not one is respectable or unhappy over the whole earth.

In theory, no Christian could accept so gloomy a view. Optimism is, surely, essential to a faith based on the gospel—the very word gospel means good news. In her early decades the Church was optimistic; despite unending persecution, Peter and Paul were happy and hopeful men. Augustine admitted his sins but his sorrow was never morbid; his *Confessions* are not chiefly concerned with his failings but proclaim God's loving-kindness towards him. The lovely old Easter hymn, the "Exultet," gives Adam and Eve their acquittal and describes their fall as a "happy fault." So much for the theory but, when it comes to practice, Christians have proved as gloomy as the rest.

Here is a contradiction for which I can find no answer; an inconsistency which Christian pessimists need to correct. It is difficult to ignore the note of gloom struck by so many orators and writers in the various branches of the Christian faith. The variety of religious experience has proved to be a variety of fears and scruples, panic about salvation, threats of damnation, a morbid preoccupation with men's sins. How explain such a Dismal Desmond approach? Was too much attention paid to the apocalyptic passages in the Scriptures; were the prophets of gloom themselves passing through a time of crisis; or could it be that the great revivalists discovered, as the journalists have later, that crowds turn out to hear bad news? Whatever the reasons, in certain epochs the emphasis was on punishment for sinners, on all that is wrong with the world. The picture of George Fox tramping the streets and crying aloud, "Woe to the bloody city of Lichfield," is no caricature.

Last year, in Washington, D.C., I shook hands with the distinguished Capuchin, Father Sebastian, whose lectures have been delighting thousands over many years. Indeed, I sought him out after American friends, living in Britain, had told me of the benefit they had derived from a course of lectures entitled "What Is Right with the World." Father Sebastian drew this happy approach from the right sources, the books and verses of G. K. Chesterton.

Chesterton was by temperament an optimist. Once, years ago, a Portuguese doctor who was driving me to Fatima gave me a quotation which I have never been able to trace. Braking his car vigorously in a narrow lane, my friend remarked with due solemnity, "As your Mr. Chesterton said, 'An optimist guesses right as often as a pessimist but he is much happier.'"

Chesterton, however, was not just a cheery soul who viewed the world through rosy glasses; he was, among modern writers, the supreme theological optimist. In a poem entitled "The Pessimist" he fills up the verses with the joy of the incarnation but begins and ends brusquely:

> You, that have snarled through the ages, take your answer and
> go–I know your hoary question, the riddle that all men know.[2]

The charm of Chesterton's optimism lies in his forthright acceptance of sin. He was humble enough not to be surprised by his weakness or to attribute the blame to other agencies. We often attempt this. We complain about our heredity, environment, teachers, clergy, doctors, even our psychiatrists. "You are responsible; you gave me the excuse for behaving badly," wrote an angry patient to her psychotherapist. Chesterton was very happy to blame only himself. On the very day when he was received into the Catholic Church and at the moment when he was making his first confession, a friend, waiting for him in another room, scribbled on a piece of paper, "He joined the Church to restore his innocence. Sin was almost the greatest reality to him. He became a Catholic because of the Church's practical power in dealing with sin."

The wisdom and insight of G.K.C. is seen in his wholehearted acceptance of sin as inevitable in man. Here for him was both tragedy and triumph, the risk that had to be taken, the pain that had to be suffered for the greatest experiment known in our creation, man's freedom of choice. Evolution was less to the fore in Gilbert Keith Chesterton's day. All the advances in this field should have thrilled him, for evolution adds to the story of Adam and Eve a more profound meaning at the moment when the last of the hominoids reached that point of consciousness when it could stand back, judge a situation, and choose for itself. The first free creatures on earth made the wrong decision, but Chesterton saw in this a profound advance. He wrote of Adam:

When Adam went from Paradise,
He saw the sword and ran;
The dreadful shape, the new device,
the pointed end of Paradise,
And saw what Peril is, and Price
And knew he was a man.

Many have said as much before, nor is this the whole story, but Chesterton had a unique, intuitive, and penetrating point of view. Some would see him as an uncanonized saint, all who know his works would accept that he was a mystic, a point brought out by his dear friend Maisie Ward in her great biography. His preoccupation was with the fall of man and the challenge behind it, leading to a second Adam, the Son of God made man.

I was pleased that Maisie Ward judges as "one of his most brilliant illustrations" a passage of his which helped me much in my schoolboy days. We may speak, says G.K.C., of a manly man but not of a whaley whale. "If you want to dissuade a man from drinking his tenth whisky, you slap him on the back and say, 'Be a man.' No one who wishes to dissuade a crocodile from eating his tenth explorer would slap it on the back and say, 'Be a crocodile.' For we have no notion of a perfect crocodile; no allegory of a whale expelled from his whaley Eden." This passage if taken seriously, and it is very serious, would give us the answer to Walt Whitman's gloomy verdict on mankind. For we have an image of a perfect man and the chance to attain it and the power to pick the means to achieve this end. Animals commit no sin but they have no higher standards, no will-to-meaning, no personal goal.

I must have been ten years old when I first saw G. K. Chesterton in the Church of Our Lady of Victories, High Street, Kensington. My father took me into this old church to pray and as we walked up the side aisle to the Lady Chapel, he tapped my shoulder and whispered in my ear. I gathered that I was not to stare or to turn round quickly but that there was a very famous man just behind me on a chair. I would like to tell you that he was wearing his cape and his curious pince-nez, but memory is deceitful after fifty years. This I recall, that the chair looked small and the occupant enormous and that if he had not been frowning, I would have judged that he was asleep. Dates are now hazy but I would guess that Chesterton became a Catholic some two years later and very soon afterwards wrote his *Orthodoxy*. Maybe it was the plan for this which made him frown.

Maisie Ward maintains that *Orthodoxy* is by far the most personal of Chesterton's writings, that it is "his history of his own mind." That it is a remarkable and most encouraging book, I agree after several readings, and would recommend it to anyone in search of meaning who finds himself bogged down. One particular passage deserves particular attention because it answers poor Piggy's question, "What makes things break up as they do?" Indeed, in a paragraph or two, Chesterton explains the flaw in Adam and Eve, deals with the Pharisee praying in the temple, begins to emphasize the importance of confession, and reveals unwittingly both his optimism and his humility. For me, this passage brings back nostalgic memories of the London of my boyhood, when Hanwell enjoyed a peculiar reputation thanks to its enormous mental home. Chesterton's second chapter, "The Maniac," opens thus:

> Thoroughly worldly people never understand even the world; they rely altogether on a few cynical maxims which are not true. Once, I remember walking with a prosperous publisher who made a remark which I had often heard before; it is, indeed, almost a motto of the modern world. Yet I had heard it once too often and I saw suddenly that there was nothing in it. The publisher said of somebody, "That man will get on; he believes in himself." And I remember that as I lifted my head to listen, my eye caught an omnibus on which was written "Hanwell." Said I to him, "Shall I tell you where the men are who believe most in themselves? For I can tell you. I know of men who believe in themselves more colossally than Napoleon or Caesar. I know where flames the fixed star of certainty and success, I can guide you to the thrones of the Supermen. The men who really believe in themselves are all in lunatic asylums."
>
> He said mildly that there were a good many men after all who believed in themselves and were not in lunatic asylums. "Yes, there are," I retorted, "and you of all men ought to know them. That drunken poet from whom you would not take a dreary tragedy, he believes in himself. That elderly minister with an epic from whom you were hiding in a back room, he believes in himself. If you consulted your business experience instead of your ugly, individualistic philosophy, you would know that believing in himself is one of the commonest signs of a rotter. Actors who can't act believe in themselves; and debtors who won't pay. It would be much truer to say that a man will certainly

> fail because he believes in himself. Complete self-confidence is not merely a sin; complete self-confidence is a weakness. Believing utterly in one's self is an hysterical and superstitious belief like believing in Joanna Southcote; the man who has it, has Hanwell written on his face as plain as it is written on that bus."
>
> And to all this my friend, the publisher, made this very deep and effective reply: "Well, if a man is not to believe in himself, in what is he to believe?" After a long pause, I replied, "I will go home and write a book in answer to that question." This is the book that I have written in answer to it.

G. K. Chesterton wrote his book and lived his life to combat the one, insidious, psychological heresy, practiced by those who believe in themselves. Adam and Eve were the first, followed by billions, including King David, the Pharisee in the temple, Judas Iscariot, the prep school kids on a desert island, Adolf Hitler, you and me. G. K. Chesterton delighted in man's basic weakness, for he knew that those who stand on their own two feet are heading for disaster; every idol has feet of clay. St. Paul said as much. Writing to the Corinthians, the apostle recognized the danger of pride. To keep him from believing in himself, God had given him "a thorn in the flesh," a chronic debility, which the experts have interpreted differently. Paul carried with him throughout his life some physical or moral weakness, impurity, epilepsy, anxiety: the nature of this thorn is anybody's guess but the purpose of such a trial Paul well understood. "About this thing, I have pleaded with the Lord three times for it to leave me but he said, 'My grace is enough for you; my power is at its best in weakness.' So I shall be very happy to make my weaknesses my special boast so that the power of Christ may stay over me and that is why I am quite content with my weaknesses and with the insults, hardships, persecutions and the agonies I go through for Christ's sake. For when I am weak, then I am strong."

Though he probably never guessed it, G. K. Chesterton had the good news of the gospel woven into the fabric of his mind. In a truly Christian style he denounced the hypocrites, the do-gooders, the people who believed in themselves. He said to them and especially to one of them, "Chuck it, Smith." But if he attacked the establishment men, the puritans, the self-righteous, he did this to defend the dignity and freedom of those who did not believe in themselves. So he loved the people who had not spoken and the rolling English drunkard who made the rolling English road. It was typical of G. K. Chesterton to write a poem in honor of dust and to end it with this triumphant stanza:

> When God to all his Paladins
> By his own splendour swore
> To make a fairer face than heaven
> of dust and nothing more.

Shortly before his death, Chesterton came upon T. S. Eliot's "The Hollow Men." In this he read of the deep and morbid pessimism of the newer generation, expressed in the lines

> This is the way the world ends,
> This is the way the world ends,
> This is the way the world ends,
> Not with a bang but a whimper.

After reading this Chesterton wrote: "Forgive me if I say in my old-world fashion that I am damned if I ever felt like that . . . I knew that the world was perishable and would end but I did not think that it would end with a whimper but, if anything, with a trump of doom. I will even be so indecently frivolous as to burst into song and say to the young pessimist:

Some sneer; some snigger; some simper;
In the youth where we laughed and sang.
And *they* may end with a whimper,
But *we* will end with a bang."

Maisie Ward who knew G.K. so well ends her biography with this detail and sums up his ambitions thus: "His last message for this generation was the sound of the trumpet calling us to Resurrection. A dead world must find life again, must go back to the meaning of Genesis." It is because this great man gave Adam and Eve their due, saw the dignity of man in his very weakness that I have given him a place of honor in this book.

5. Show me the way to go home

We may miss the point of Christ's story if we call it the parable of the prodigal son.[1] In the first place, Christ was not drawing our attention to the boy but to his father; secondly, this son was a wastrel and prodigal only in the uncomplimentary use of that word. Thanks to the parable, the word "prodigal" has come to mean repentant and this the boy in the parable never was. Preachers and hymn-writers often harp on the deep sorrow of the prodigal but this the boy himself never expressed.

Do you remember that famous old hymn which we used to sing at parish missions:

God of mercy and compassion,
Look with pity upon me;
Father, let me call Thee Father,
'Tis Thy son returned to Thee.

It was a good hymn, but one thing is certain, the prodigal son did not sing it as he set out on his return journey; his mood would have been better covered by "Show Me the Way to Go Home." As St. Luke tells us, he came to his senses by the pigsties and his sorrow amounted to no more than this: "How many of my father's paid servants have more food than they want and here I am dying of hunger."

Too much emphasis on the sorrow of the son obscures the vital lesson which Christ was trying to teach. This parable is of unique importance, for only one man in history had the knowledge and authority sufficient to attempt such a comparison. I see no reason why others could not have thought out some other of Christ's parables, the sower, for example, or the good Samaritan. Teresa of Ávila, Thomas More, C. S. Lewis, and other imaginative writers produced excellent parables in their day. But when it comes to sin, even the holiest of the saints would know only the sinner's reactions and maybe this is why the prodigal son has been treated so well. One man alone had firsthand knowledge of God's reactions to the sinner and his sin. In this parable, more than in any other, we acquire an insight into God's line of thought.

The story of the prodigal son is grouped with two others, for Christ thought the moral so important that he repeated it three times. And he began with a simple human instinct, known to all his listeners, to reveal, of a sudden, that such a reaction is also divine. How astonishing to invite a crowd of sinful people to examine their own feelings if they want to know God's attitude to those who have sinned. He began by asking, "What man among you?" before describing the behavior of the shepherd who leaves ninety-nine sheep in the wilderness because he discovers that one has strayed. He would not have put the question, had he not known that every farmer in the audience would have done the same.

While the farmers pondered the thought, he turned to the women: "What woman with ten drachmas would not, if she lost one, light a lamp and sweep out the house and search thoroughly until she found it? And then when she found it, call together her friends and neighbors: 'Rejoice with me,' she would say, 'I have found the drachma I lost.'"

This method of teaching a vital lesson proves especially

effective, for we have each experienced such a reaction in ourselves. Few of us now deal with sheep or share the shepherd's anxiety, but many of us have our pets. Recently I had to recall the woman who dropped the drachma, for I mislaid the cap of my fountain pen. Others joined me in the search out of kindness with an enthusiasm much less than my own. The cap could not be found and a neighbor offered me another, for he had two. I thanked him without saying that I did not really want his cap but my own. Eventually we called the search off, I persuading myself that the lost cap was old and battered and that I rarely used that pen anyway. When the searchers had all left and I was ready for bed, I began the hunt again. I pulled out the furniture, turned out my pockets, searched every drawer. No doubt the psychiatrists have a name for the compulsion which drives an elderly priest in his pajamas to rummage in the garbage cans in the middle of the night. Does it sound fanciful to suggest that, in the back of the mind, there lurks a personal sense of duty towards anything that belongs to me?

So the fountain pen cap was retrieved soon after midnight and I slept peacefully. Indeed, my first thoughts on waking were not for God or myself but for the miscreant top. I experienced real joy and satisfaction in having saved it but, after so much fuss, I have to chuckle, for I have not used that pen since.

Presumably, you are not so nutty but you may have experienced the same. In all cases of loss, it pays to analyze one's feelings, for it was to these that Christ appealed in his effort to tell us about God. Simone Weil, who makes her points with the fewest number of words, has this to say in her comments on the *Paternoster:* "He is Our Father; there is nothing real in us which does not come from Him. We belong to Him. He loves us since He loves Himself and we are His."[2]

Here, surely, is the exact truth, the theme that lies behind the incarnation, the key point, the only point in these three parables. Admittedly it takes some swallowing. Theologians and philosophers agree that if there is a supreme being, he must *be* supreme. Were God to lack anything, he would have to surrender his divinity. How can he need or yearn for me? Yet here we have Christ, in three precise parables, teaching what seems to be the opposite. Christ attributes to the infinite God the very sentiments of the housewife sweeping her house, of the shepherd searching for his sheep, of myself in pajamas at midnight sifting the garbage for the top of my fountain pen. Could we solve the problem by presuming in God those three dimensions which we have in ourselves? May we say that God does not need us but he does want us; this was the situation of the father in the story of the prodigal son?

Christ's three stories are carefully graded to bring out the three situations in which a man wants his own. The coin was an inanimate object, the errant sheep had movement and was stupid, the prodigal, when he set out to waste his father's money, chose such a course deliberately.

It would be foolish to attempt a comment on this famous story in so short a space. It is, however, important to study the psychology of a sinner and, as one modern writer puts it, this parable "calls forth all the resources of psychology." Indeed, Salvatore Garofalo has done us a great service by analyzing the behavior of the younger son. He writes:

> From the very beginning, the striking thing about the story is the insolence of the younger son: *Father, give me the portion of the substance which falleth to me*. The cruelty and finality with which the younger son leaves his home are emphasised by a number of details: *not many days after*—perhaps just long enough to find a buyer; *gathering all together went abroad into*

> *a far country,* which in Hebrew meant a land beyond the seas, thus opening an abyss, as it were, between father and son. The prodigal makes this clean break in order to see life; and there wasted his substance, living riotously. In other words, he wasted what his father had given him, for it was in fact a gift, not an inheritance; the prodigal made no effort to make his own personal fortune nor to show his own constructive ability, nor to use his new independence to develop a more forceful personality. He put as much distance as possible between himself and his father with the sole aim of escaping all advice and control.[3]

There is value in recalling these small details, given by Christ that we may preserve a right proportion between the malice and insolence of the boy in the story and the extreme triviality of many of the small sins which we confess. And when we come to the distinction between mortal sin and venial sin, we need to keep in mind the fate of this wastrel whose sin almost brought him to his death. Salvatore Garofalo brings this out excellently, when describing the prodigal in his distress.

> This, then, is what sin is; a betrayal of a father's love and protection, the abuse of his gifts, abandoning home, the squandering of one's possessions, and the loss of one's dignity; humiliation, misery, hunger; the total destruction of a man, an existence worse than death itself.

Let us leave the boy here. You may side with those who maintain that in his misery he repented; I feel that he said no more than "It will pay me to go home." You may think that the speech which he rehearsed en route showed true contrition; I see it as no more than the best way of getting round the old man. Had he been able to find a new job or another patron, he would not have returned. There was nothing generous or gentle about this boy. What does it matter, for the parable concerns the father, who saw him a long way off, ran out to meet him, cut into his speech, gave immediate orders for a banquet, not because the son was sorry but from joy that something lost had been found. In our era of broken homes and generation gaps, such a situation is not uncommon; I know any number of parents who would have their child back at any price.

Every now and then, questions are put to me about humor in religion and why it is that, in the gospel, there are few jokes and no laughs. There are one or two who must have laughed, the Samaritan women, Matthew and the other publicans who sat down with Jesus for dinner, and the Best Man at Cana when the best wine was kept to the last. We know that the Eastern mind differs from ours and recall that, in the days before printing, all documents were handwritten; one can appreciate the unwillingness to waste precious effort on a few trivial Ha Ha's. But if laughter is restricted to Abraham and his wife—and theirs was cynical—we meet in the gospel a far more enduring happiness, namely, joy. Joy is one of the virtues most frequently recorded in the gospel, a point often overlooked.

The first mention of joy is found at the very start of St. Luke's gospel for, when Mary visited Elizabeth in the hill country, the babe in Elizabeth's womb jumped for joy. And when the baby was born, all her friends and neighbors, hearing of the Lord's kindness, "hurried round to share her joy." To the frightened shepherds at Bethlehem the angel gave this message: "Do not be afraid, listen, I bring you tidings of great joy, a joy to be shared by the whole people. Today, in the town of David, a saviour has been born to you; he is Christ, the Lord."

Christ himself often spoke about joy, as in that lovely passage: "A woman in childbirth suffers because her time has come, but when she has given birth to the child she forgets the suffering in her joy that a man has been born into the world." In the very same homily at the last supper, Christ promises to share with us his joy: "But now I am coming to thee; and while I am still in the world, I am telling them this so that my joy may be theirs and reach its full measure in them."

A striking fact which should never be forgotten is that Christ speaks most often of joy when he is dealing with the forgiveness of sin. So in these three parables about sin, the atmosphere is joyous and the shepherd who has found his sheep invites his neighbors to come and rejoice with him. The housewife who recovered her silver piece probably spent double the amount on light refreshments. "Rejoice with me," said she to her neighbors, "I have found the coin that was lost." At the end of this second parable, Christ made a baffling statement: "I tell you this, there will be more rejoicing in heaven over one repentant sinner than over ninety-nine virtuous men who have no need for repentance."

I used to think that such a statement was a little unfair. I used to wonder why the shepherd would risk his flock to chase after one maverick. Mine was the mentality of the elder brother of the prodigal when he heard the sound of music and dancing as he trudged home after a hard day in the fields. Was Christ suggesting that it was better to be a sinner, that God preferred sinners to the just who kept away from sin? The father of the prodigal gave the answer when he went outside to pacify the indignant boy. He never said that he loved the prodigal more; he never condoned his sin or spoke about forgiveness. All that he could say was that he, as a father, could not suppress or contain his joy: "It was only right we should celebrate and rejoice because your brother here was dead and has come to life; he was lost and is found."

Joy, then, is the word most often used in the gospel to describe God's reaction to one who repents. To judge by St. Augustine's approach, the sacrament of penance, as we now call it, should be the happiest of the sacraments. All too often it is not. Had our ancestors only named it the sacrament of forgiveness, we might have been spared some of its gloomier overtones. The funereal faces in the confessional queue bring back the memory of schooldays and the long wait outside the headmaster's room. Or to watch the struggle, sometimes lasting for several years, before a man can bring himself to go to confession is to suspect that many Christians have in mind a different type of father from the one who welcomed the prodigal home.

Has this lack of joy in the sacrament come from the Church, from individual priests, from teaching in school, from an alien, puritan background which has so gravely affected Christians in the English-speaking world? No doubt we are all partly to blame—penitents, clergy, teachers—that the gospel joy of forgiveness has been obscured. Confessionals are dingy, penitents look resentful, priests appear bored. Compare the exhilaration of Augustine, the exuberance of G.K.C. when it came to forgiveness, with the true but depressing description of his first confession given by such a sincere and spiritual writer as Graham Greene. Greene made his first confession when he was received into the Church in Nottingham in 1926:

> The first General Confession which precedes conditional baptism and which covers the whole of a man's previous life is a humiliating ordeal. Later we may become hardened to the formulas of confession and sceptical about ourselves; we may only half intend to keep the promises we make until continual failure or the circumstances of our private life finally make it impossible

> to make any promises at all and many of us abandon confession and communion and join the foreign legion of the Church and fight for a city of which we are no longer full citizens. But in the first confession, a convert really believes in his own promises. I carried mine down with me like heavy stones into an empty corner of the Cathedral, dark already in the early afternoon, and the only witness to my baptism was a woman dusting chairs. I took the name Thomas, after St. Thomas the doubter, and not Thomas Aquinas, and then I went on to the Nottingham *Journal* office and the football results and the evening of potato chips. I remember very clearly the nature of my emotion as I walked away from the Cathedral; there was no joy in it at all.[4]

How sad the transition from the joy of that father, slaying the fattened calf, to Nottingham Cathedral, "dark already in the early afternoon." Chesterton became a Catholic in 1922 "because of the Church's practical power of dealing with sin." Chesterton was joyful and he made his first confession "in a kind of shed with a corrugated iron roof and wooden walls —part of the Railway Hotel, for at that time Beaconsfield had no Catholic church." Four years later Graham Greene, equally sincere, no less earnest, underwent the same experience and walked away with "no joy in it at all."

With the father of the prodigal in mind together with Christ's constant emphasis on joy and rejoicing, one becomes aware that something in our modern ritual of penance is wrong. If this is borne out in Graham Greene's sad account, it is further underlined in the behavior of those scrupulous people for whom confession is an agonizing exercise. One good thing may be said about the prodigal, he was not scrupulous. With such a father, he did not need to be. Yet in certain periods of Church history scruples were very much in fashion, and a tender or delicate conscience was much prized. Scruples normally pertain to the second dimension and are a certain symptom of the divided self. They are not basically religious and one meets innumerable scrupulous people with no beliefs of any kind. One poor soul, whom I met recently, would test the lock on the back door six or seven times a night.

No one has better described the convulsions of a religiously scrupulous person than Sir Thomas More. Sitting in his cell in the Tower of London, awaiting execution, the Man for All Seasons wrote one of the best accounts that I have read. This passage should restore our joy in forgiveness by giving us a chance, if we are scrupulous, to laugh at ourselves. The man who wrote it had death just around the corner and that final moment when he would put all his trust in God.

> Thus fares the scrupulous person who frames for himself more than double the fear that he needs and many times a greater fear when there is no cause for fear at all. Of that which is no sin at all, he makes a venial sin; that which is venial, he imagines to be mortal, and yet, for all this, continues to fall into them because of their very nature they are things that no man can live long without.
>
> Next, he fears that he is not fully and properly confessed, nor never fully contrite and, then, that his sins will never be forgiven him; so, then, he confesses and confesses again to the burden both of himself and of his confessor. Then, every prayer that he recites, though he said it as well as the frail infirmity of man will suffer, yet he is not satisfied unless he says it again and, after that, again. And when he has said one thing thrice, he is as little satisfied with the last as with the first and, then, his heart is forever heavy and restless and in fear, full of doubt and dullness without comfort or spiritual repose. With this fear of the night, the devil sorely troubles the mind of many a right good man and reduces him to some great inconvenience. For he will drive him if he can so much to think of the rigours of

God's justice that he will keep him from pondering on the comfortable remembrance of God's great mighty mercy and so make him do all his good works wearily.[5]

A great many holy people are troubled by scruples for a time. Even saints as balanced as St. Teresa of Ávila, St. Ignatius of Loyola, and St. Francis de Sales were plagued with anxieties and scruples in the first stages of their spiritual advance. The depression vanished for good when they came to know Christ more intimately and worried less about themselves.

Let Augustine end this chapter for he, perhaps, more than any other saint, came to confession through joy. Yet he on his own admission and for many years had been a deliberate sinner, had no doubts about his past transgressions; his need for forgiveness in the present moment was a red-hot reality. His *Confessions* are a nonstop dialogue with God. He saw that forgiveness requires such a dialogue between two persons in the third dimension, heart to heart. Dare we presume such an intimate relationship with God?

Augustine had doubts at first at a moment of great sadness when an intimate friend died:

> That huge load of misery which was first to be lightened and afterwards removed by thee, O Lord, lay heavy upon me. I knew it but I would not, or could not, seek the remedy because when I thought of thee, it was not anything substantial or firm that came into my mind; nor was it thou but my own vain imagination and error which was, indeed, my God at that time. Whither was it possible for my heart to fly from my heart? Whither could I escape from myself?[6]

In the end, a sudden appreciation of Christ's three parables changed Augustine's attitude to sin. He asks God what there is in man that gives God more joy in forgiving a sinner than in dealing with the just who need no forgiveness and, next, almost as though he had heard the answer, he exclaims: "We listen with joy whenever we are told of the lost sheep carried home on the shoulder of the shepherd, rejoicing; and when the coin is restored to thy treasury, her neighbors rejoicing with the poor woman who found it."

It is Augustine's theory that joy has no meaning without sorrow, that the greater the pain before it, the greater the joy. Thus sailors rejoice when a storm is over and men best enjoy food who were hungry before.

> A friend is sick and his pulse threatens danger; all who long for his recovery are sick in mind with him. He is restored though he walks not with his former strength; yet there is such joy as was not present before, when he walked sound and strong. Of the return of the prodigal, he says to God with so much feeling, "The joy of the house brings tears to our eyes."

6. A lesson from Littlemore

An obvious temptation faces any author, the urge to arrange things neatly under points one, two, and three. By such a device he may gain precision, but life itself is rarely so orderly. Writing about confession, my thoughts may be tidy; inside the box, if I ever get there, I am speechless, muddled, and in tears.

As already pointed out, the psychologists like to arrange their findings under headings one, two, and three. Thus their analysis of man reveals him simultaneously in three dimensions, identified by Dr. Frankl as the physical, mental, and spiritual. Writing about human motivation, the same author gives us the will-to-pleasure, the will-to-power, and the will-to-meaning; another neat arrangement inside a triangular frame. From other psychologists we are offered three levels, three ways of life, three tapes, three recordings, and, who knows in the not too distant future, three blind mice.

The same mystic number three turns up in theology whenever the sacrament of penance is discussed. As children we knew that contrition, confession, and satisfaction were required and in the old "Confiteor" we dutifully struck our breast three times and admitted that we had sinned exceedingly in thought, word, and deed. As likely as not, the priest would then say, "For your penance say three Hail Marys," to which one timid child answered, "Father, I only know one."

Some people place great store on mystic numbers, St. Augustine one. Years ago, I remember rubbing my eyes in South Chicago when a rabbi, recovering from surgery, attributed his cure to the numbers on his theater trolley which matched some mystical figures supplied by the prophet Daniel. Who knows? Points one, two, and three are somehow all linked to our three dimensions and show how important these may be. One day, when we join St. Paul in the third heaven, we may discover how our three dimensions derive from the three persons of the Trinity.

After laughing at such a neat arrangement, let me offer you a final one, two, three. This last triplet proves of great practical value when considering the subject of sin. For sin may be approached from three angles, and we have a legal, a theological, and a psychological view of sin. Any muddle in our minds between these may produce great sorrow and anxiety. This I have seen in many questions about confession that have been put to me. These questions stem from a basic query, expressed by different people differently. One questioner put it neatly: "What I say in confession is not what is wrong with me." Another will word it: "I don't feel sorry; I cannot believe that God would take my list of peccadilloes seriously." Those of delicate conscience blame themselves: "I must be a hypocrite; I seem unable to examine my conscience properly." Statements such as these suggest some confusion between the legal, theological, and psychological views of sin.

In our present transitional age, with attitudes swiftly changing, a further worry appears. Those who ask questions about confession often add a postscript: "I used to go to confession often but now I seem to be falling away." To the distaste of going to confession is added a sense of guilt for not having been. Yet the frequency of going to confession may be viewed legally, theologically, and psychologically. A sinner who sincerely tries to fulfill the legal or theological requirements may psychologically be confessing far too frequently. These and other worries may be discussed in later chapters but here let us give our attention to contrition, the basic quality needed for the forgiveness of sin. One must think this out for oneself.

I found no better way of satisfying myself about these three approaches than that of studying the gospel scene. The world may have changed but sin remains the same.

(1) No one who reads the gospel can miss the legal view of sin. The scribes and Pharisees, not wholly to their discredit, knew, loved, studied, and defended the Mosaic law. Those who today clamor for an unstructured Church should remember that the rules and regulations imposed by Moses were revealed to him by God. Societies flourish in the first, physical, dimension and cannot survive without laws. The Pharisees were not wrong in recognizing this. On such issues as adultery, ritual washings, Sabbath day observance, they studied the traditions and issued guidelines so that the law might be understood. As with lawyers in any age, some used the law to line their own pockets, to feather their own nest. Christ denounced those who were hard on others and did not observe the law themselves. Both he and St. Paul respected the law; they found it wooden but this did not mean that it was wrong.

After the destruction of the temple and the sack of the holy city, exiled Pharisees fled to the township of Jamnia to resume their researches again. Josephus, apostate and Pharisee, who went to Rome and gained an impressive reputation, secretly admired his old-time colleagues and their brave persistency.

In the Church of today we, too, have our lawyers and moralists. As Newman wrote, "We are guided in our ordinary duties by the books of moral theology which are drawn up by theologians of authority and experience as an instruction to our confessors . . . Reducible as these directions, in detail, are to a few and simple heads which I have mentioned, they are little more than reflections and memoranda of our moral sense, unlike the positive enactments of the Legislature."[1] How many of those lists of sins which we were taught as children derived from this good but academic source.

(2) While the scribes and Pharisees continued to debate how many fresh eggs a man could carry on the Sabbath, Christ and St. Paul were unfolding to the world a vast and impressive theology of sin. Why, John the Baptist was preaching forgiveness before Christ had said a word. To identify himself with sinners, Christ stood in the queue to be baptized. From then until his death, forgiveness of sin was to be for him a central subject, the very heart of the liturgy of the last supper from which all Christian liturgies derive. Two thousand years later, at Mass every morning, I say, "This is the chalice of my blood, the blood of the new and everlasting covenant, which will be shed for you and for all men so that sins may be forgiven." Calvary, the sacraments, the Mass, the very concept of sacrifice, from the days of Abraham down to the great epistle to the Hebrews, derive their meaning and purpose from the theology of sin.

(3) A third approach to sin in the gospel story was hinted at earlier in this book. The psychology of each sinner, in that strange, obscure world of the third dimension, proves all-important where sorrow and forgiveness are involved. Let that prostitute who entered the Pharisee's house while Christ was at table represent every other sinner who has been drawn towards him. She was sobbing but not because she had broken the law of Moses in any legal sense. Had this been the worry, she could have consulted the Pharisee, presiding at the dinner, for he could have rattled off the regulations for her defilement to be erased. But, as we read in the epistle to the

Hebrews, such rules were insufficient, they could not "bring any worshipper to perfection in his inner self; they are rules about the outward life." She stood there weeping; her needs were far deeper than that. She was not interested in the legal view of sin nor was it an interest in theology that brought her sobbing and uninvited to this hostile dining room.

At the center of her heart—we may judge this by our own —was an awareness of her weakness, misery, and failure and, behind such pain, a relief that she had met someone so understanding that she could be herself and give herself away. In her profession, she hired out her first dimension but her heart needed more than cash. Behind all the misery and squalor of every type of sin remains a grain of hope. Christ kindled and revivified such flickering hopes.

It helps me greatly to analyze such gospel situations as this. I note that she said nothing, confessed nothing but revealed everything. She had no need to recite any act of contrition, for her tears were more eloquent than words. In plain words, she did no more than summon up sufficient courage to do something about her desolate situation, to run down the street, gate-crash a door, run weeping into a righteous dining room. Her tears were her acts of contrition. Francis de Sales in a conference went even further. He remarked, "A sigh may be enough."

She never saw or guessed Christ's view of the picture, seated as he was as the guest of honor in a righteous and hypocritical home. He saw her tears and felt the disapproval; he said to his host, "Much has been forgiven her because she has loved much." In this bewildering situation, of first-dimensional impersonations, only Christ and a common prostitute spoke heart to heart.

When Christ said, "I am the Way and the Truth and the Life," he covered all three dimensions, showing us the way to behave in the physical world around us, the truth for our mental dimension and a new and fuller life in the heart. That frightened, unwanted girl, who sobbed but said nothing, yearned for this fuller life and little more. The Pharisee watched the scene with scorn from the center of the high table, wondering how a human being could bring herself so low. But, as Newman wrote of sinners, "They rise by falling. Plainly so, for no condescension can be as great as that of Our Lord himself. The more they debase themselves, the more they are like to him, and the more they are like to him, the greater must be their power with him."

No need here to repeat the whole story; enough that Christ turned to the scornful man beside him. "Simon," he said, "I have something to say to you."

This scene long baffled me. I thought I knew everything about contrition, having practiced it and preached on it for years. I knew, for example, that sorrow must be in the present moment or not at all. We may be sorry for the past but our act of sorrow must be a spontaneous reaction, in the third dimension, at the red-hot point of consciousness. That girl was sorry in the present moment; Christ saw her weeping now. I knew that, though memory is a precious gift–a man who loses it becomes half a cabbage–it cannot be trusted to give me an exact picture of the past. In retreats, I have often urged men and women to be sorry in the present and not to worry unduly about the details of past sins. Motives cannot be reconstructed or reweighed. There are acts which if done today would be gravely sinful but which looked harmless thirty years ago. I know now that the same could be stated the other way round. I have known for years the feeling that my friend expressed so neatly, "What I say in confession is not what is wrong with me."

Many times in conferences and retreats, I have made the

point that confession is very much easier for someone who has committed a grave sin. Were I to strike a Papal legate, I would have no problem about what to say. But bad temper, sulking, name-dropping, scrounging sound so trivial and hardly seem to justify the fuss. Yet, thanks to an unusual word by Cardinal Newman, the counting up of small sins now makes sense. Newman was describing the way in which the thoughts and ideas of individuals are absorbed by society as a whole. He writes of them being percolated, a word familiar to all of us who like our coffee fresh. "Doctrine, too," says Newman, "is percolated, as it were through different minds."[2] The description helps me greatly for, even with each individual, a kind of percolation is perceptible. Take the case of that weeping girl; she probably knew nothing of theology and yet, in her heart, had absorbed the story of Adam in a strained, filtered, or vaporized form. In our own case, the legal approach to sin and the theological view of sin are not recognizable in the third dimension but, in a percolated form, they play their part.

The image of the percolator helps us to make sense, an unpleasant sense, of our trivial, weekly sins. They do not add up to much, they cannot be recalled or identified, but the resultant cup of coffee in the third dimension leaves a very bitter taste in the heart.

I think I learned more about sin from Newman than from any other source. For Newman directs our attention not so much to sin as to God. He accepts the role of the priest as judge and adviser but insists in the spirit of King David that we confess our sins primarily to God. "For I am well aware of my faults, I have my sin constantly before my mind, having sinned against none other than you, having done what you regard as wrong." Such an attitude, basic to confession, is, I think, threatened in the modern Church. We have come to regard confession as a burden, imposed by the Church. For some it is no more than a liturgical ritual or a counseling session which is sometimes helpful but more often not. Among some, there is the view that sin is not an individual but a community weakness and that we sin chiefly against our fellow men.

Newman pulls us up with a start. He pens, I suggest, a picture of that Pharisee who scorned the poor sinner and, reading it, I came to realize how closely it resembled me:

> We find these men possessed of many virtues, but proud, bashful, fastidious and reserved. Why is this? It is because they think and act as if there was nothing really objective in their religion; it is because conscience for them is not the word of a lawgiver, as it ought to be, but the dictate of their own minds and nothing more; it is because they do not look out of themselves, because they do not look through and beyond their own minds to their Maker but are engrossed in notions of what is due to themselves, their own dignity and their own consistency. Their conscience has become a mere self-respect . . . When they do wrong, they feel, not contrition of which God is the object, but remorse and a sense of degradation. They call themselves fools, not sinners; they are angry and impatient, but not humble. They shut themselves up in themselves; it is a misery to them to think or speak of their own feelings; it is a misery to suppose that others see them and their shyness, and their sensitiveness often becomes morbid. As to confession, which is so natural to the Catholic, to them it is impossible; unless, in cases where they have been guilty, an apology is due to their own character; is expected of them and will be satisfactory to look back upon. They are victims of an intense self-contemplation.[3]

"Simon," said Christ, "I have something to say to you."

Once one starts quoting Newman, it is difficult to find any good reason to stop. I risk one further quotation for if, in the passage just quoted, Newman hits off Simon and myself, in another vivid paragraph he draws the high-class, academic outlines of that weeping girl:

> Who can deny the existence of conscience? Who does not feel the force of its injunctions? But how dim is the illumination in which it is invested and how feeble its influence compared with that evidence of sight and touch which is the foundation of Physical Science. How easily can we be talked out of our clearest views of duty. How does this or that moral precept crumble into nothing when we rudely handle it; how does the fear of sin pass off from us, as quickly as the glow of modesty dies away from the countenance, and we say, "It is all superstition." However, after a time, we look round and then, to our surprise, we see as before the same law of duty, the same moral precepts, the same protests against sin, appearing over against us, in their old places, as if they never had been brushed away, like the divine handwriting upon the wall at the banquet.[4]

And Jesus said to Simon, "I tell you, her sins, which are many, are forgiven for she loved much."

Recently I revisited Littlemore, Newman's retreat outside Oxford from 1842 to 1845. When I was an undergraduate at Oxford, nearly forty years ago, Littlemore was unbearable, a village shattered by the heavy traffic on the main London road. The traffic has now been diverted, the buildings restored, and a group of devoted people tend the garden and show one to Newman's room. I knelt in the same place as he had knelt, more than a century ago.

The saintly Italian priest who had spent five hours in the rain on the top of a coach to get to Littlemore, described the scene thus: "I took up my position by the fire to dry myself; the door opened–and what a spectacle it was for me to see at my feet John Henry Newman, begging me to hear his confession and to admit him into the bosom of the Catholic Church. And there, by the fire, he began his general confession with extraordinary humility and devotion." A note tells us that Newman finished his first confession next day.[5]

Newman, we know, to prepare for the great moment, had stayed indoors all day. He writes later, to a friend, "The moment before acting may be, as can easily be imagined, peculiarly dreary—the mind may be confused—no reason for acting may be forthcoming . . . I could do nothing but shut myself up in my room and lie down on my bed."

I knelt by the fireplace in Newman's room at Littlemore and read a thought of his, printed on a pious card: "Faith is founded on the knowledge that God is almighty; Hope is founded on the knowledge that God is all-merciful."

7. The why-therapy

Even submarines have to surface and we, certainly, cannot remain in the thrilling world of the third dimension for long. Mystics and contemplatives apart, most human beings are able to endure the solitude and nakedness for only a few minutes, in the manner of those trying their first sauna bath. Christ told us "it is from the overflow of the heart that the mouth speaks." The heart is designed to overflow like a fountain and, sooner or later, we are deposited in the second dimension with our hearts in our mouths.

In this book, we have spent many chapters underground in the third dimension because any true understanding of the gospel demands familiarity in this field. Without it, our view of Christ would be superficial and our welcome no warmer than the one he met in that Pharisee's house. But if one may study the workings of the heart without exhaustion, direct personal experience of our innermost being has to be limited. Few of us have the strength sufficient to isolate the heart and to cut it off from thought and action for long. The length of time varies very much with different people and even in the same person from day to day. Time is useless in the third dimension; the bottom of the heart is timeless so one need not attempt to measure acts of sorrow by the clock. A true act of contrition may be over in a flash.

Back in the second dimension, we are inclined to divide our prayers into neat sections as though filling sandwiches with ham. The prayer books give us acts of faith, hope, charity, contrition to be devoured one at a time. In the third dimension I find that these operations fuse into one. Augustine wrote, "The act of adoration of a sinner is an act of contrition," a view that helped me much. Years ago, I found this in the prayer of Manasses: "I bow down the knee of my heart and I adore thee"; it takes but a second to genuflect at the red-hot point of consciousness.

Conflicting attitudes to confession confront us at this point. Where the Church sees man as a whole and counts in all three dimensions, there are those who limit confession to the third dimension and like to confess their sins only to God. Luther was one of these. "To feel," "to experience" are favorite expressions of his. His basic dogma, justification by faith alone, is directly traceable to his own experience in the confessional. As one author puts it, "Seeking assurance of forgiveness, he claims to have found it neither in his own acts of repentance nor in the objective efficacy of the priest's absolution but in the acceptance by faith of God's promise to forgive." Both Luther and Calvin retain confession as a sacrament, see the seemliness of going to a minister, allow for penitential services in church. Luther adds, "Secret confession as practiced now, though unprovable from Scripture, is highly commendable, useful, even necessary." Yet the absolution of a priest achieved nothing and the contrition and confession of the penitent was unnecessary. Faith in God's promise of forgiveness is very much a third-dimensional experience.

William James, writing more than three centuries after Luther, comments on this doctrine and its sad, unexpected consequence:

> The complete decay of the practice of confession in Anglo-Saxon communities is a little hard to account for. Reaction against popery is, of course, the historic explanation, for in popery, confession went with penances and absolution and other inadmissible practices. But on the side of the sinner himself, it seems as if the need ought to have been too great to accept so summary a refusal of its satisfaction. One would think that in more men the shell of secrecy would have had to open, the pent-in abscess to burst and gain relief, even though the ears that heard the confession were unworthy. The Catholic Church, for obvious utilitarian reasons, has substituted auricular confession to one priest for the more radical act of public confession. We English-speaking Protestants, in the general self-reliance and unsociability of our nature, seem to find it enough if we take God alone into our confidence.[1]

Is it enough for the balance and happiness of the whole man to take God alone into our confidence? Much earlier in this book, I quoted the view of Dr. Paul Tournier, the devout Swiss Calvinist: "There are all around us vast numbers of people who are sick for confession." These need to take two into their confidence, God and their psychiatrist.

Luther found no assurance of forgiveness in the priest's absolution where Thomas More, Chesterton, Newman, and how many thousands of others reacted the other way round. This was brought home to me by my own father, who, in his early twenties, was received into the Catholic Church. At the time he was an Anglican on paper and, as I presume, who knew him later, full of deep thoughts. As a boy of seventeen, he volunteered and served with the Highland Light Infantry in the Boer War. A man of peace, he was to spend another four years in the trenches in World War One. He used to remind me when I was young that we cradle Catholics took confession very much for granted, having lived with it all our lives. He had not. He would describe how he would kneel by his bed at night to express some kind of sorrow, never knowing for certain whether God had forgiven him or not. Over the years, there accumulated for him what he described as a spiritual dunghill about which he could do no more than pray and keep his fingers crossed. Once inside the Church, confession for him not only lit up God's mercy but a special act of mercy, through which God permitted a man, a priest, to make a visible gesture, an outward sign of inward peace.

This is not the place to restart the battle of the texts. At the Reformation, protagonists hurled chunks of Scripture at each other with few obvious results. Reading back, it becomes clear that issue was joined on contemporary practices and abuses, not on the basic doctrine of the forgiveness of sin. Protestants and Catholics alike knew that forgiveness was essential to the gospel, that Christ forgave sins himself, on two solemn occasions passed on his power to others, which powers were used by the twelve in the very early Church. Let one example suffice here; we read in the Acts of the Apostles about the Christians at Ephesus: "Many believers came forward, confessing their evil practices and giving a full account of them; and a number of those who followed magic arts made their books into a heap and burned them in public; the value of these was reckoned up and proved to be fifty thousand silver pieces." No one would wish to argue that this incident was identical with confession as we know it today. Much more important is the fact that the Church had a practical power of dealing with sin from the very beginning and this through the agency of men. I find it moving that Luther, Calvin, and the Roman apologists, while abusing one another, had at heart the Christian spirit of mercy and the common desire to make forgiveness as easy as possible for men. Each saw in the other's point of view an imposition and a burden which Christ would never have instituted and which he would have wanted to remove. Abuses, alas, are always possible where men are concerned. But far deeper than these is the desire in man to express his sorrow in all three dimensions and to enjoy the certainty of forgiveness conveyed visibly to sinners in Christ's day.

Thousands of technical tomes must have been written about confession across the centuries. Happily I need not examine them here or quote them, for the Catholic sense of the sacrament of penance has been set out simply by St. Francis de Sales. How frequently in my lifetime has this great saint and doctor solaced me. Here, in his eighteenth Spiritual Conference he says:

> Before learning how we ought to prepare ourselves to receive the Sacraments and what fruit we ought to derive from their reception, we must first understand what Sacraments are and what their effects are. The Sacraments then are channels, through which, so to speak, God descends to us as we through prayer ascend to him, since prayer is nothing else than the lifting up of the mind and heart to God. The effects of the Sacraments are various although they all have but one and the same aim and object which is to unite us to God. By the Sacrament of Baptism, we unite ourselves to God as a son to his father; by that of Confirmation as a soldier to his captain, getting

> strength to fight and to conquer our enemies and temptations; by the Sacrament of Penance we are united to God like reconciled friends. Now, these are the different effects of the Sacraments but they all demand the union with God.[2]

This description pleases me for it underlines the union between myself and God. Next, the outward sign in the sacrament is not some type of magic but God's share in a dialogue. There can be no doubt that God is able to forgive us our sins without confession; the need for an outward sign is on our side, not on his. Thirdly, could there be a better title than the sacrament of reconciled friends?

Writers as sensitive as de Sales and Newman approach confession in a spirit which is less and less common today. Ours is a penal approach, a schoolboy attitude, that we have been caught, we must confess because the Church so tells us; it is easier to get it over and take our punishment. Were we, for a moment, to recall the joy of the gospels, we would appreciate far better the reunion of reconciled friends. Newman retained this joy and liked to quote the words of his dear friend Keble: "Friends do not ask for literal commands; from their knowledge of the speaker, they understand his half-words and from love of him they anticipate his wishes." Francis de Sales, stressing the right intention needed for confession, returns to the desire of union with God and to "rendering ourselves more pleasing to him, without any admixture of private interest." The sacrament of reconciliation should mean much more than rattling off a shopping list of small offenses; it is the sacrament for those who know their own weakness and who do not believe in themselves.

As the question of what to confess proves an enduring problem to many people, we should, perhaps, consider it here.

We may ask St. Francis first and his immediate answer is rich in common sense:

> I would not have you so scrupulous and anxious about confessing numbers of trifling imperfections, since we are not even obliged to confess venial sins if we do not wish to. If however we do confess them, we must firmly resolve to amend, otherwise it would be an abuse of confession. Nor must we torment ourselves when we cannot remember our faults so as to confess them, for it is incredible that a soul who frequently examines herself should not have noticed sufficiently any faults of importance as to remember them. As regards these many but trifling defects, you may speak to the Lord about them whenever you perceive them; an act of self-humiliation, a sigh, will be enough for that.

If you were God, what kind of confessions would you be pleased to hear? Such a question is not blasphemous for, if you recall, Christ began his three parables of forgiveness by asking the people, "Which one among you would not feel the same?" Surely the point of the incarnation is that Christ as a man saw things in our way. Which mother among us does not know joy and satisfaction when a toddler says sorry spontaneously and in a sincere way? Which wife has not felt "if only he had told me openly"? In every human relationship there are grades of reconciliation and an ascending order of sympathy. I hardly have to eavesdrop in our supermarket to hear the old gossips writing this paragraph for me. Such clichés as "No, dear, I can feel no sympathy for him"; "Well, she brought it on herself but I must say that she is making an effort"; "If you knew what I know about them, you'd make allowances"; "Yes, I know he talks big but he does not really mean it," provide an accurate guide to Christ's way of thought. There was no character in the gospel whom Christ did not want to forgive. Yet he felt no sympathy at all with that servant who, forgiven a large debt, prosecuted another for a debt which was small. He showed small sympathy for Herod, much sympathy for Pilate, loved Martha without heeding her grumbling because Mary was not helping with the work. What Christ wants in confession is what he wanted also in the gospel, the sincere and contrite heart.

A priest sitting in the confessional, as I have done over thirty years for heaven knows how many thousands of hours, comes to see the sacrament from Christ's point of view. He knows very well that all who enter the confessional, himself included, want to be sincere. He comes to appreciate this portmanteau sacrament designed to cover worries of any size. Newman took two days over his first confession, and St. Ignatius of Loyola records in his autobiography, "When he came to Montserrat, after much prayer, he made a written general confession of his sins with the confessor's consent and spread it over three days."[3] Readers may think that such would not happen in our day and how wrong they would be. At certain, unexpected moments in life, often in times of sorrow, failure, fear, or crisis, a person is drawn to face reality. Alcoholics Anonymous knows this well. One of the most touching moments in my priestly life came with a young man of twenty-four, not a Catholic, who wished to join the AA or a similar organization. He had been asked to fill in a survey of his life, find a minister of religion and go through it with him. The interview took three hours. When he had gone, I found myself trembling with shame and confusion, never having attained to such sincerity as this.

If the sacrament is designed to cover cases of this kind, it is also suited to the needs of good, untroubled people, to Martha, Mary, and Lazarus. These have little to say but yearn to make the gesture; their sorrow is in their feet as they enter the box. Some, of course, come to confession, as they also went to Christ, for less worthy motives, self-pity and resentment; in a roundabout way, they confess not their own sins but the wrongs that others have done to them. Such cases are rare. Over the years, I have watched simple, quiet people attain to great holiness through the strength which this sacrament provides.

One lesson I have learned as a confessor from my experience as a penitent: never shrug off or belittle the small faults which people choose to confess. Should a confessor say, "There is nothing in that," or "Don't bother to confess this," the heart of the penitent sinks. On one memorable occasion, I confessed a small sin and the priest said, "I'm glad you confessed that; it is worth watching," and I left the box unexplainably happy and refreshed.

Some complain dolefully, "What's the use, Father? I say the same old things week after week." To which I would like to answer, "Aren't you lucky; wouldn't it be slightly awkward if you had a brand-new line every time?" The plain fact is that the choleric, the sanguine, and the melancholy stand a very good chance of confessing the same sins all their lives. There are, too, sins which those of a certain temperament will never have to confess. I could never confess that I have been lazy; it is precisely this not-being-lazy that is wrong with me.

I am determined to introduce an old friend, Theodore Parker, at this point. I came upon him in 1946 in William James's *The Varieties of Religious Experience.* He interested me so much that I pieced together biographical scraps about him, culled chiefly from *Chamber's Encyclopaedia* of 1901. More than a century ago, Theodore was saying to the people of Boston what many, myself at one time included, are thinking today. Theodore Parker was a distinguished Unitarian minister, a graduate of Harvard, who worked in the Roxbury area of Boston in 1836. In the War of Independence, his grandfather had held a command at Lexington. Theodore, we are told, drew three thousand people weekly to his sermons at Melodeon Hall and at the Boston Music Hall. Sadly enough, this great revivalist developed consumption; a lecture tour in Europe failed to help him and he died in Florence in 1860 when he was just fifty years old.

The thousands who packed Melodeon Hall of a Sunday evening went home happy and encouraged by such eloquence as this:

> Orthodox scholars say that, in the heathen classics, you find no consciousness of sin. It is very true–thank God for it. They were conscious of wrath, of cruelty, avarice, drunkenness, lust, sloth, cowardice and other actual vices and struggled to get rid of these deformities: but they were not conscious of "Enmity against God" and did not sit down and whine and groan against non-existent evil. I have done wrong things enough in my life and do them now; I miss the mark, draw the bow and try again. But I am not conscious of hating God or man or right or love and I know there is much health in me; and in my body even now there dwelleth many a good thing in spite of consumption and St. Paul.[1]

The robust common sense of Theodore Parker encouraged me greatly, many years ago. If parents suffer for a child who runs itself down, lacks confidence, and courts failure, so, surely, God derives small pleasure from mock humility. Here is the mentality of Uriah Heap, of that craven steward in the gospel who from fear of failure buried his talent in the ground. Not a few people feel it necessary to exaggerate their uselessness and sinfulness. Theodore was not one of these, nor was St. Paul, who gladly admitted that he had fought a good fight and done pretty well. To overdo our sinfulness, to see failures everywhere will rob us of the joy of a reconciled friend.

Many years ago, in Belgium, lived a very holy priest with a high reputation for sanctity, named Père Petit. By chance two other priests with the same surname lived in the same community. One evening, the porter came to the common room to announce that Père Petit was wanted in the parlor and the superior asked, "Which Père Petit?" "The holy Père Petit," said the porter, at which the holy man stood up and said, "That's me."

Theodore Parker was right to find much good in himself but we must hope that he avoided the other pitfall for, if he believed in himself, he would have repeated Adam's mistake. Indeed, he would almost be back in the temple with that Pharisee who thanked God that he was not as other men. St. Paul, who loved to boast of all that he had suffered, knew very well the source of true humility. As he told the Corinthians: "We are the earthenware jars that hold this treasure, to make clear that such an overwhelming power comes from God and not from us."

Our utter dependence on God's grace is often forgotten by those who believe in themselves. Our confessions would seem less trivial if we assumed a more positive attitude. We do not confess because we are rotten but because we are weak. In many a gospel scene, the sinner needed encouragement as much as forgiveness and all went home refreshed. Those who say, "I do not go to confession; it does not do me any good," are talking through their hats. The saints confessed frequently and doffed their hats.

With one more comment on his cheery outlook, we may leave Theodore Parker for good. When he remarks, "I am not conscious of hating God," I would like to ask him, "Whoever is?" Over the years, I have never met anyone who was conscious of "hating God or man or right or love." The answer to Theodore Parker and to those with him lies in the legal, theological, and psychological views of sin. We have met these before. The legal attitude to sin as a breach of the law, grave or trivial, is covered by the canon lawyers and moralists. Next, we see sin in a theological sense, an offense against God first committed by Adam and repeated by every sinner since. In the theology of sin we see Christ die on Calvary. The catechism, quoting St. Paul, says, "Our Saviour died for our sins and those who sin grievously 'crucify again to themselves the Son of God, making him a mockery.' " In such a theological setting, it might possibly make sense to say that a grave sinner may be conscious of deliberately rejecting God.

Finally, we have the psychological approach to sin and in this lies the answer, for here we are conscious of choosing ourselves in place of God. This aspect the gospel teaches well. When Christ died on Calvary few if any of the perpetrators were conscious of hating God or even of hating Christ himself. Even the chief priests only wanted him out of the way to safeguard their establishment. When Caiaphas remarked, "It is expedient that one man should die of the people," he gave us the perfect word on which our examination of conscience should be based. Judas never hated Christ or God but he wanted money; Peter loved his master but his own safety more. Pilate did no more than wash his hands of the whole business, passing the buck to Herod, who only wanted fun. John Mark–if that was he–simply decided that it was safer not to go back to get his garments; he fled naked down the street.

In a sense, these were all trivial sins with no hatred in

them, sins which we ourselves commit by day. Had the sacrament of penance been in existence, Peter, in the three years before that cowardly denial, would have been scratching his head outside the box and wondering what on earth he could say.

One man alone stopped thinking of his own interests on that grim evening; with incredible bravery Judas went back to the priests, admitted his sin in public and threw the tainted money to the ground. Then, sadly enough, in panic, forgetting the three parables of forgiveness, he took his life.

I have called this chapter "The why-therapy" to preserve a most useful piece of advice. It was given to me by an old Marist Father in New Zealand; if I remember rightly, at the lovely town of Timaru. We were speaking about confession and he remarked that he had found it helpful, after a penitent had accused himself of something, to ask him why. I am unable to recall his exact words but the point of his theory was that many of us begin by confessing the wrong sins. When asked, "Why did you do this?" we shed our prepared formula and get down to the truth beneath. So, should a child confess, "I have been naughty," the New Zealand Marist would ask him why. Many kids used to be thrown into confusion because they were spouting a formula by rote. Every now and then a child would pinpoint the real fault and the situation. "Because I had to go to bed when we were playing a game." Here is an imaginary setting for a grain of truth.

Let me apply the "why-therapy" to a number of fictitious situations, all of which, I hope, mirror the realities of life. Thus one mother may confess, "I am very impatient with the children," and were I to ask her why, she would say, "Because they are so naughty," to which I would rejoin, "Such impatience with naughty children may well be more a virtue than a vice." A second mother says the same and if I ask her why, she answers, "I am impatient because I am so tired," and my "why" to this reaches halfway to the truthful answer; she says, "We to go to bed too late at night." Were I brave enough to toss up another "why" I might get one or all of four honest answers: (a) TV (b) Bingo (c) Entertaining (d) My husband likes to go to the pub at night. And a "why" to these four might disclose whether she is treating the children fairly; whether she has committed a sin or not.

Outside confession and for the sake of this book I asked a friend to name his greatest worry and he replied immediately with scant reflection, "I love her but in recent years I have unending squabbles with my wife." Looking suitably holy, I lobbed up a little "why?" Said he, "I really don't know, Father. I suppose because she is always nagging at me." A third "Why?" produced a series of spluttered excuses, that his wife was a darling but overpious, a bit narrow-minded, something of a shrew. A fourth "why" was not required; of a sudden he sat up straight and remarked in the flat, formal tones of a TV announcer, "I drink too much."

In the gospels, the "why-therapy" is much in evidence. Judas asked, "Why should not this ointment have been sold for three hundred pence and given to the poor?" but St. John gave the true answer. "Now he said this not because he cared for the poor but because he was a thief." Were we to ask, "Why did the prodigal go home?" St. Luke tells us, "He came to himself and said, 'How many hired servants in my father's house abound with bread and here I perish with hunger?'" When the five foolish virgins arrived late at the wedding and banged on the door, they no doubt said, "We were delayed, we had to buy oil for our lamps." Had I been posted at that door, I would have asked them, "Why did you have to buy oil?"

The supreme example of the "why-therapy" begins in the gospel when Christ asks, "Why do you see the speck in your brother's eye and not the beam in your own?" Across the centuries, how very few have come anywhere near the true answer, given by Cardinal Newman; his "I see the speck in my brother's eye because I hate my brother" made me grasp how, unwittingly, dishonest I have been.

Sin which is divided into mortal and venial on the legal level in the first dimension, becomes the mockery of Christ on Calvary in the second dimension with which theology is concerned. As with coffee beans, the conclusions from these two dimensions percolate to the third. In the nebulous world of the third dimension all our "whys" are answered without words. Here we join in honest, open company with Pontius Pilate, Peter, Herod, Mary his mother, Judas, and the neighbors across the road. I long for the moment when I can ask Pilate, "Why did you wash your hands?" With Judas, who was so brave, the only "why" would be, "Why did you lose courage at the end?" I would ask Simon the Pharisee, "Why did you invite Christ to dinner in your house?" Zacheus, "Why did you climb that tree?" the Samaritan woman, "Why did you tell the whole village?" Mary his mother, "Why did you stand by the cross until the end?"

Herod the King would, in the third dimension, answer, "the will-to-pleasure," Pilate, Caiaphas, and many others would use that most honest and treacherous of words "expediency." Zacheus would, surely, admit that, as a short, middle-aged man, the climbing of a sycamore tree was in itself abhorrent but "the will-to-meaning" made the effort worthwhile. Mary his mother, faced with a "why," would have answered, "I love him" and here we reach the very peak of a human heart.

When I go to confession today, I examine my conscience with the aid of five words, all scriptural: "expediency," "cowardice," "pleasure," "power," "joy." Were you to see me in the confessional queue and to ask me, "Why are you going to confession?" I would have to answer, "I have seen the beam in my own eye."

8. The wind of change

Though sanity, happiness, and peace are meaningful only in the present moment, few resist the temptation to live ahead. So today prophecies about life in the eighties are two-a-penny in newsprint and on the TV screens. We read about furniture for the eighties, socialism in the eighties, air travel through the eighties, with Big Brother due to arrive in 1984.

In contrast to this, the sacrament of penance in the nineteen eighties should remain very much as it is today. At heart and in the third dimension, human beings show little change. Our impersonations on the stage vary with current fashions but conscience does not alter and the causes of sin remain the same. Thousands of years ago, the same will-to-power that we know led Cain to kill his brother, and the-will-to-pleasure persuaded David to interrupt his psalm writing to commit murder and adultery.

Normally, when reading the Bible, we need to rely on commentaries and footnotes to understand the ancient Hebrew weights and measures, their farming habits or their currency. No notes, however, are required where sin is concerned. The letter which Paul wrote to Corinth and its Christian community could be posted today to the Christians of Kensington, London, Kensington, New Brunswick, and Kensington, Maryland. We picture the early Christians as saints, breaking bread and singing Alleluias, but Paul was the man on the spot. He writes to the Corinthians in advance, "What I am afraid of is that when I come, I may find you different from what I want you to be . . . and then there will be wrangling, jealousy and tempers roused, intrigues and backbiting and gossip, obstinacies and disorders. I am afraid that on my next visit, my God may make me ashamed on your account and I shall be grieving over all those who sinned before and have still not repented of the impurities, fornications and debauchery they committed."[1]

Men do not change very much. Years ago Ronald Knox, in his *Essays in Satire,* wrote a brilliant essay on the "New Sin."[2] As I recall the story, a learned professor announced that he had discovered a new sin and would disclose it at a public meeting. Needless to say, the Royal Albert Hall was jammed to the doors.

In this final chapter about sin and confession, it may prove helpful to consider the question of change. I find it imperative to face up to change, to distinguish the peripheral from the essential, to become like the householder in the gospel "who brings out of his treasure what is new and what is old."

King Solomon it was who coined the cynical expression "There is nothing new under the sun." To our brave new world with its new deals, new looks, new maths, new morality, new horizons, the preacher in Ecclesiastes has an old and timely message to convey. King Solomon sees us going round in circles like the wind which starts in the south, veers to the north and back again.[3] Or like the raindrops which swell the rivers, are carried out to sea only to go back and begin again, "What was, will be again; what has been done will be done again and there is nothing new under the sun. Take anything of which it may be said, 'Look, this is new.' Already long before our time, it existed. Only no memory remains of earlier times;

just as in times to come, next year itself will not be remembered." St. Paul would gladly endorse this view. It was the constant cult of the new that so disgusted him in ancient Athens. "The one amusement the Athenians and the foreigners living there seem to have," wrote St. Luke later, "apart from discussing the latest ideas is listening to lectures about them."

There is nothing new under the sun, save the various changes of the backcloths against which men play their many parts. We have man on a camel, man on a horse, man in a car, man in a jet, man in a sky-lab, man on the moon. If only we could eliminate men, everything would be new. I still chuckle at an advertisement in an eighteenth-century journal, stating that a certain Señor Jumpedo would, on a certain Sunday, in Vauxhall Gardens, perform the extraordinary feat of jumping down his own throat.

There is nothing new under the sun and yet King Solomon might have wanted to amend his statement had he had the chance of meeting Christ. When you come to think of it, Christ effected a bewildering revolution, the like of which will not be seen again. He gave us everything new, a new covenant, a new birth, to each the chance to slough off the old and to become a new man. His teaching is still new after two thousand years, his sacraments still effective; men still leave home and parents to become his disciples, for his sake men are still ready to lay down their lives. As St. Justin the Martyr put it, "No one has so believed Socrates as to die for the doctrine he taught; no one was ever found undergoing death for faith in the sun."

In an earlier chapter, I introduced Christ as a great psychiatrist. The risk was considerable but worth taking in an age in which so many people depend for balance on their psychotherapist. Christ was much more than a psychologist or faith healer, but this was the side of his character that so many saw first. We watched him drawing to himself many sad, sick, and sinful people, not by bribes or political inducements, but by understanding and sympathy. If he failed with the crowds that wanted to make him king, he was highly successful with a wide variety of individuals, a Pharisee, a prostitute, several fishermen, two tax collectors, a Roman centurion, a permissive Samaritan housewife, and, at the very last moment, a repentant thief.

I called him a psychiatrist, for his approach was personal and inward, penetrating the layers of makeup and impersonation to reach the clown behind the masks. In the isolated world of the heart, where guilt and fear are both endemic, those who met Christ regained a will-to-meaning through his personal love. When Augustine wrote, "Because you loved me, you made me lovable," he touched the deepest point in the human heart.

This, however, is only part of Christ's story, though, sadly enough, I meet many who see no further and who go through life with only half the truth. These are devoted people, drawn to Christ personally, dependent on him as one may be drawn to a doctor, a teacher, a professor with whom one "clicks." With Nicodemus, they go to him alone and after dark. They treasure his words, imitate his every gesture, obey all his precepts so that their left hand does not know what their right hand is doing as they turn the other cheek. Some are mystics, all are Christ-like, but are they Christians in the fullest sense? I suggest that they are covered by the Oxford Dictionary in a secondary definition of a Christian as "one who follows the precepts and example of Christ."

I have to ask myself if this is the whole story and would Christ have been satisfied with imitation of Christ. Here I am not thinking of Thomas a Kempis' great book, so badly named from the opening words of its first chapter; Professor Allison Peers wanted to see it called "The Book of Friendship with Jesus," very much nearer to the point.[4] The imitation to which I refer is that done in monkey or parrot fashion, the kind of adulation which might have satisfied Bunthorne or Adolf Hitler but never Christ.

In the shortest possible space, for this is no Scripture lesson, I would like to consider in Christ four unusual traits. These, I find, not only help in confession but throw a new light on the imitation of Christ.

(1) Though Christ in his lifetime had power, he had no will-to-power, a point brought out on Good Friday in his dialogue with Pilate and on the previous evening when he washed the apostles' feet. "Tell me, which is the greater, the man who sits at table or the man who serves him? Surely, the man who sits at table; yet I am here among you as your servant." In the training of the first apostles no other subject was raised more often than this.

(2) Christ never used his power to compel anyone to obey him; always the other party had to take the initiative. He seemed to want each friend to act freely and to be himself. Devoted parents and teachers show similar restraint, that the children may develop, not into yes-men, but into men. Hence in the parables which so closely reflect Christ's mind, the emphasis is on initiative and resourcefulness. Even the unjust steward was commended for living by his wits. The two who took the risk and traded with their talents were richly rewarded; as was the merchant who sold all to buy the pearl of great price. Only the timid servant who, for fear of failure, buried his money in a napkin was severely rebuked.

(3) Though Christ knew all about the heart and the third dimension, he was in practice the complete realist. Though he told us that it is from the overflow of the heart that the mouth

speaks, he never saw words as all-important; eventually the heart is revealed as good or bad in the first, physical dimension by the valid test of deeds. "It is not those who say 'Lord, Lord' who will enter the kingdom of heaven but the person who does the will of my father in heaven." One parable, already quoted, puts Christ's teaching in a nutshell; the son who refused to work in the vineyard, then changed his mind and went there, loved his father more.

(4) Understanding human beings as he did, Christ recognized that sorrow and forgiveness must involve the whole man. Sorrow in the heart but not overflowing is as fruitless as a puddle of rain. When Christ dealt with sinners, he catered for all three dimensions, indeed he gave the first clues to that contrition, confession, and satisfaction which Christian tradition later would enshrine. The model confession in the gospel was made by Zacheus. Without being asked, the little publican said, "Here and now, Lord, I give half of what I have to the poor; and if I have wronged anyone in any way, I make restitution of it fourfold." Jesus turned to him and said, "Today salvation has been brought to this house." Poor Judas also acted spontaneously in the first dimension, throwing back the tainted money. He said, "I have sinned in betraying the blood of an innocent man." We have, too, the first trace of a firm purpose of amendment: "And Jesus said to the sinful woman, 'Neither do I condemn thee; go away and do not sin anymore.' "

When facing the winds of change which whistle around my confessional box, I cling to these essentials and let the rest be carried away. If I interpret Christ's mind correctly as he reveals it in the gospel, I must be myself in confession, take the initiative, judge myself entirely on the deeds I have done. All three dimensions want to be involved. Contrition in the heart, confession through mind and tongue, reparation in the physical dimension, these are my concern. The firm purpose of amendment is not as firm as it should be but here Christ promises assistance from outside. The very point of each sacrament is the grace and courage which it was designed to provide. The visible outward sign, made with Christ's authority, gives comfort and assurance to the whole man.

One fact is clear in Christ's lifetime, that the apostles never grasped the meaning of the resurrection or took his words about it seriously. Who can blame them when faced with an occasion unique in history? The excitement of Easter itself and the sudden outpouring of strength on the first Whitsunday compelled them to see Christ and to recall his teaching in a new, three-dimensional way. Thus the breaking of bread, which must have seemed pointless to them on Good Friday evening, now assumed an overwhelming significance. Again, the promise, twice made, that they would forgive sins took on a new and bewildering meaning, when, on Easter Sunday, Christ appeared in their midst. St. John, who was a witness, tells the story simply:

> The disciples were filled with joy when they saw the Lord and he said to them again, "Peace be with you. As the father sent me, I am sending you." After saying this, he breathed on them and said, "Receive the Holy Spirit. For those whose sins you forgive, they are forgiven; for those whose sins you retain, they are retained."

Earlier in this chapter, I quoted from the dictionary a secondary definition of a Christian as "one who follows the precepts and example of Christ." Such a description may have covered those who knew Christ before he died on Calvary but after Easter Sunday this was no longer adequate. The full definition of Christian becomes, after Pentecost, "one believing in, professing or belonging to the religion of Christ."

Such a definition would have been new even to the apostles until the Holy Spirit opened their inward eye. Now they no longer followed Christ or imitated Christ but they professed and belonged to his religion; they became the founder members of his Church. And at the very center of this Church, as representing the epitome and essence of his earthly mission, were those two great mysteries, the breaking of bread and the forgiveness of sin. Vast mysteries indeed; inconceivable—that is, beyond the range of human imagination; incomprehensible—out of reach of human reason; and yet taught by a simple Galilean to simple people two thousand years ago.

Here we are concerned with one of them, the forgiveness of sin through the sacraments of baptism and penance, the latter known to St. Jerome and others as "the second plank."

The story of this sacrament makes fascinating reading; through it we may watch the mercy of Christ unfolding across the ages and adapting itself to the needs of each succeeding century. History offers reliable guidelines to those buffeted by the winds of change. It sifts the essentials from the nonessentials or, to put it better, the eternal from the transient. If we want to foretell the future, we have only to glance backwards, for there is nothing new under the sun.

Which practices in the ritual of confession may be termed transient? The question of public or private confession might be one. The fashion today is for groups, be they pop, political, or penitential, and this mentality matches the mood of the first Christians in apostolic days. Small, close-knit communities, sharing all in common, the early Christians found public confession and public penance a joy. If our modern penitential services convey Christ's mercy and forgiveness so much the better for us all. What fun we have in store if we return to the ritual described by St. Gregory the Wonderworker, with sinners in grades—mourners, hearers, kneelers, and bystanders—doing their *thing* around the Church.

The early Christian experiment did not last. It fell to pieces in the centuries of persecution when many frightened Christians left the Church. Later these sought forgiveness, and bitterness ensued, comparable to the hatred of collaborators by resistance leaders in Europe after World War Two. Absolution was refused, and un-Christian rigorism was sponsored, chiefly by men who, later, left the Church. The Christian Church rejected such harshness and the secrecy of the confessional was adopted for the penitent's sake. Auricular confession—as it is sometimes called—is thought to have originated in the sixth century, introduced by Irish monks.

The confessional box is transient and there are rumors that soon it will be removed. We take it for granted but, in fact, it is a recent piece of ecclesiastical furniture. St. Charles Borromeo is said to have thought it out and it appeared in the middle of the seventeenth century, fitting the precise, decorous spirit of the Council of Trent. Further, it afforded scope for elaborate decoration when baroque architecture was at its peak. The confessional box was functional but certainly not essential; we may confess and gain forgiveness anywhere. With a little bit of luck, our last and most significant confession will be in bed. In his *A Priest in Stutthof* the Lithuanian, Father Yla Stasys, describes the practice of confession in a Nazi concentration camp. Polish women, complete with mops and disguised as charladies, sought out the priest in a disused store. "Even though the window already sparkled like crystal," each penitent polished it as she told her tale.

If the confessional box is decorative but unimportant, the same may be said of the various formulas for confessing which men have used. Any number of these which once found favor have now disappeared. Language is forever expanding and changing and the words of an act of contrition which satisfied our grandparents sound ponderous to us today. Whether or not the new rite of confession will prove more apt or more enduring is anyone's guess. The new penitential services annoy some people but give others relief. At best, they attempt in liturgical form to dispose us, to lighten the burden of self-examination which once we had to attempt by ourselves. I see this danger in some of them, that they lessen our sense of individual guilt. By using the word Sin in the singular, not the plural, we escape our personal responsibility. Such a subtle change of grammar is common and intentional in a world obsessed with community. If we say with John the Baptist, "Behold the Lamb of God," it makes a difference whether he takes away the sin or the sins of the world. Dr. Karl Menninger in his *Whatever Became of Sin?* makes the point well: "If a group of people can be made to share the responsibility for what would have been a sin if an individual did it, the load of guilt rapidly lifts from the shoulders of all concerned." There is no true alleviation in such a ploy. The genuine need for personal guilt and personal sorrow safeguarded, new rites and up-to-date liturgies are helpful but peripheral.

One further important item in the ritual of confession seems to me transient. Were it possible to question Christians from each century about the frequency of their confessions, we would need a computer to sift, sort, and catalogue the conflicting replies. Who now knows the habits of sixth-century Celtic monks, of the early desert fathers, of the sturdy pilgrims of the *Canterbury Tales?* It is generally maintained that the first Christians, as adult converts, had small need for confession, their sins were forgiven at baptism. Confession as "the second plank" came later when, after baptism, things went wrong. The frequency or infrequency of confession varies with different people, turns on the three dimensions, is much affected by temperament, environment, even by nationality. The precept of the Church that we should confess at least once a year was not promulgated until A.D. 1215. It applies to those who have committed grave sin, is purely disciplinary, and, according to Suárez, could be altered at any time.[5] That the Church has the authority to make such laws, that much wisdom lies behind them, does not alter their transience.

In deciding the frequency of confession, I have found it helpful to recall the three attitudes to sin. Legally, confession is available at any time, and the Church may legislate that all should go at least once a year. Theologically, the sacrament gives strength as well as pardon and frequent confession proves an abiding joy. Psychologically, we may need advice on the matter but, in the end, we each of us must decide. The present decline in the number of confessions may be a symptom of laxity or it may show a growing maturity in those who were urged to go too often when they were young.

There is nothing new under the sun. I was reared in a devout Catholic home in which confession was infrequent but taken very seriously. Indeed, when, as an earnest young priest, not long ordained, I assisted an old aunt at her death bed, I asked if she would like confession, she answered sweetly, "There is no need, I went last month." At boarding school, frequent confession was first put before us, with no compulsion, merely encouragement. Frequent communion had been introduced and it was thought seemly to confess one's sins in preparation for the Eucharist. So one confessed frequently in term time, rarely in the holidays. As a Jesuit novice, frequent confession became a habit, a sign of piety. I remained a middle-of-the-roader where some colleagues would confess two or three times a week. One settles down peacefully over the years. Now, in the middle sixties, I am back to where I was in early childhood, for the trip to Penzance by helicopter costs too much.

If so much is transient in confession is there anything permanent? To this I would answer with Christ's question at the last supper, "Tell me, which is the greater, the man who sits at table or the man who serves him? Surely the man who sits at table, yet I am here among you as your servant." Poor Peter was embarrassed that Christ should demean himself, and ours should be the same reaction, for these words are not restricted to the last supper but apply in every confessional box. Permanent is the love of Christ and permanent his attitude of service to each sinner; there is no compulsion in the confessional. He wants me to be myself, to take what initiative I like, to engage all three dimensions, to feel the relief of tearing off the mask.

Surely no more curious court of law is known to man. In what other tribunal is the culprit allowed to accuse himself? Even with my devoted parents, I was told what was wrong with me. No police car has ever signaled me to put the question "Would you like to own up to anything?" Only in confession am I defendant and prosecutor; the magistrate is a sinner like myself.

Chesterton in his *Autobiography* put this well:

> When people ask me, or indeed anybody else, "Why did you join the Church of Rome?" the first essential answer, if it is partly an elliptical answer, is "to get rid of my sins." For there is no other religious system that does *really* profess to get rid of people's sins. It is confirmed by the logic, which to many seems startling, by which the Church deduced that sin confessed and adequately repented is actually abolished; and that the sinner really does begin again as if he had never sinned . . . the ac-

cumulations of time can no longer terrify. He may be grey and gouty; but he is only five minutes old.

G. K. Chesterton's story of his life turns on sin and confession and the recapture of innocence:

> I have found only one religion which dared to go down with me into the depths of myself. I know of course that the practice of confession, having been reviled through three or four centuries and through the greater part of my own life, has now been revived in a belated fashion . . . In short, I would not be supposed to be ignorant of the fact that the modern world in various groups is now prepared to provide us with the advantages of Confession. None of these groups, so far as I know, professes to provide the minor advantage of Absolution.

I have often been asked, "What does it feel like to hear confessions as a priest?" Let Newman's lovely passage serve as my reply:

> How many are the souls in distress, anxiety or loneliness whose one need is to find a being to whom they can pour out their feelings, unheard by the world? Tell them out they must; they cannot tell them out to those whom they see every hour. They want to tell them and not to tell them; and they want to tell them out, yet be as if they be not told; they wish to tell them to one who is strong enough to bear them yet not too strong to despise them; they wish to tell them to one who can at once advise and can sympathise with them; they wish to relieve themselves of a load, to gain a solace, to receive an assurance that there is one who thinks of them, and one to whom in thought they can recur, to whom they can betake themselves, if necessary, from time to time, while they are in the world . . . If there is a heavenly idea in the Catholic Church, looking at it simply as an idea, surely, next after the Blessed Sacrament,

> Confession is such. And such is it ever found in fact—the very act of kneeling, the low and contrite voice, the sign of the cross hanging, so to say, over the head bowed low, and the words of peace and blessing. Oh, what a soothing charm is there, which the world can neither give nor take away.[6]

In the confessional I feel like an unjust steward but one who has cleared it with his master; I ask, "How much do you owe my Lord?" and you say, "A hundred quarters of wheat," to which I answer, "Here is your bill, quick, sit down and write it as fifty."

Notes

So slight a book should not be asked to carry footnotes, lacks sufficient names to justify an index, and might appear pretentious if saddled with a bibliography. Yet, as a serious work, it should respect the needs of readers who require references. These short notes provide additional information for those who would like to pursue the subjects further for themselves.

1 Guilty, O Lord

1 Dorothy Sayers wrote feelingly about Christian forgiveness in her *Unpopular Opinions,* p. 14 (Victor Gollancz, London, 1946).

2 Those interested in the penitential practices of primitive peoples should consult *Sin, Its Reality and Nature; a Historical Survey,* edited by Pietro Palazzini and Salvador Canals Navarrete (Scepter Publishers, Dublin, 1964). In the opening article, Giuseppe Graneris writes on the "Concept of Sin in Comparative Religion," with elaborate notes on source books.

3 Dr. Paul Tournier has practiced medicine in Geneva since 1928. Later he acquired psychiatric training and experience "because he learned that many of his patients needed help going deeper than drugs or surgery." Of the two quotations in this chapter, the first is from his *The Meaning of Persons,* p. 115 seq.; the second may be found in *A Doctor's Casebook in the Light of the Bible,* p. 209. (Both books are published in paperback by S.C.M. Press, London.)

4 Professor A. W. Reed describes the writing of Thomas More's *Four Last Things* in his introduction to More's *English Works*

(Eyre and Spottiswoode, London, 1932). The actual text here quoted is from Rastell's first edition of his uncle's *Works* (1557).

2 Out of the depths

1 Dr. Viktor Frankl, *The Doctor and the Soul,* Introduction, p. ix (Bantam Books, New York, 1967).

2 St. Teresa of Ávila, *The Interior Castle* (Image Books, Garden City, N.Y.), p. 37; vol. 2 of the *Complete Works of St. Teresa,* p. 207 (Sheed and Ward, London, 1963).

3 Dr. Thomas Harris, *I'm OK–You're OK* (Harper & Row, New York, 1969). The book is described as a practical guide to transactional analysis. It caused quite a stir at the time of publication and has helped many since.

4 Thomas More composed his "Seven Stages of Man" for his own pleasure, when he was still young enough to be living in his father's house. This youthful attempt was first published by Rastell in 1557, a few years before Shakespeare was born. It would be interesting to know if Shakespeare knew of this work and used it. The poet's father was a stanch Catholic and one of his schoolmasters became a Jesuit. The quotation about the actor on the stage, given here, is taken from vol. 1, p. 479 of More's *English Works.* More's description of prayer may be found in his *Life of Picus, Earl of Mirandola,* English Works, vol. 1, pp. 347–48.

5 Archdeacon Grantly's busy morning is described in *The Warden,* p. 116 (Everyman's Library, New York).

6 William James appears frequently on these pages. I quote only from his *The Varieties of Religious Experience,* of which there are two paperback editions, Fontana Books and Mentor Books. Daudet's words may be found on p. 173 (Fontana Books, London).

7 Augustine, *Confessions,* p. 68 (Fontana Books, London), on man laughing alone; p. 167, slightly modernized, on the certainty of free will. Also available in Image Books, Garden City, N.Y.

8 F. Sherwood Taylor; *Two Ways of Life,* p. 35 seq. (Burns, Oates and Washburne, London, 1947).

9 Tournier, *The Meaning of Persons,* p. 159.

3 Jesus Christ, psychiatrist

1 I trust I am right in omitting the chapter and verse of every gospel text. Such references may easily be traced and I am hoping that sufficient detail is given in the narrative to make each incident clear. Certain key passages affecting this chapter may be listed here. (a) The story of the Pharisee praying in the temple may be found in Luke 18: 9–14. (b) The disciples were told to pray and fast in secret, Matthew 6. (c) St. Peter's great act of sincerity is found in John 21. (d) The good tree bringing forth good fruit is recorded in Luke 6: 43; two verses later we learn that it is from the overflow of the heart that the mouth speaks. (e) The incident caused by the disciples eating without first washing their hands is most fully reported in Mark 7.

2 For the will-to-pleasure, will-to-power, etc. of Dr. Viktor Frankl, *The Doctor and the Soul,* Introduction, p. x. Dr. Frankl, a psychotherapist of international fame, spent several years in a Nazi concentration camp; his first book, *Man's Search for Meaning* (Washington Square Press, New York, and Hodder and Stoughton, London, 1963), in a grim setting, shows what the search for meaning involves.

4 Thank you, Eve

1 William Golding, *Lord of the Flies,* pp. 154, 223 (Faber and Faber, London). Also available in Capricorn Books, New York.

2 *The Collected Poems of G. K. Chesterton* (11th edition, Methuen & Company, London). I have quoted from "The Pessimist," p. 352; "In Praise of Dust," p. 356; "On Righteous Indignation," p. 184. Also from *Orthodoxy,* ch. 2, *The Maniac,* p. 15 (Image Books, Garden City, N.Y., 1959), and the *Autobiography* (Hutchinson & Co., London, 1937). The final chapter, "The God with the Golden Key," sets out G.K.C.'s views on optimism, pessimism, and confession. I quote from p. 341, and from Maisie Ward, *Gilbert Keith Chesterton* (Sheed and Ward, London), p. 396, for G.K.'s first confession; p. 176 for his views on the fall; p. 546 his plea for Genesis.

5 Show me the way to go home

1 The three parables here mentioned are set out together in Luke 15.
2 Simone Weil, *Waiting on God,* pp. 166–67 (Fontana Books, London).
3 Salvatore Garofalo provides his detailed study of the prodigal in his article "Sin in the Gospels"; cf. *Sin; Its Reality and Nature* (Scepter Publishers, Dublin, 1964), pp. 63–65.
4 Graham Greene, *A Sort of Life,* Pocket Books, New York, 1973.
5 Thomas More, *A Dialogue of Comfort,* pp. 244–45 (Everyman's Library, New York, 1962). *A Dialogue of Comfort* was written by Thomas More in the Tower of London, awaiting trial and death. It says much for the faith of this remarkable man that this, his last book, penned in a grim situation, contains so many of his best quips and jests. As Professor Chambers put it in his *Thomas More,* p. 299 (Penguin Books, Baltimore), "More's writings in the Tower are more carefree than those which he wrote in freedom; a collection of More's merry tales would draw heavily from the *Dialogue of Comfort.* There is a marked contrast between the happiness of the *Dialogue* and the grim tone of *The Four Last Things,* written when More was rising to power in the King's service."
6 Augustine, *Confessions,* p. 98, on his first sorrow; p. 197 seq. on his joy.

6 A lesson from Littlemore

1 Newman, *The Allegiance of Catholics and the Primacy of Conscience; a Reply to Mr. Gladstone,* p. 360, *A Newman Reader* (Image Books, Garden City, N.Y.).
2 Newman, *Development of Christian Doctrine,* p. 365 (Longmans, Green & Co., New York, 1927).
3 Newman, *The Idea of a University,* pp. 203–4 (Image Books, Garden City, N.Y.).
4 Newman, "Sermon on Christianity and Medical Science," *The Idea of a University* (Image Books, Garden City, N.Y.), p. 460.
5 Meriol Trevor, *The Pillar of the Cloud,* pp. 358–59, gives the details of Newman's reception into the Church (Doubleday & Company, Garden City, N.Y., 1962).

7 The why-therapy

1 William James, *The Varieties of Religious Experience,* p. 443, on confession; p. 95 for the views of Theodore Parker, quoted later.
2 Francis de Sales, *Spiritual Conferences,* p. 347 (Burns, Oates and Washburne, London, 1906).
3 Ignatius of Loyola, *The Testament of Ignatius Loyola,* p. 69 (Sands & Co., London, 1906).

8 The wind of change

1 2 Cor. 12: 19–21.
2 Ronald Knox, *Essays in Satire,* p. 113 seq. (Sheed and Ward, London, 1928).
3 Ecclesiastes 1:6–11.
4 E. Allison Peers, *Behind That Wall,* p. 42 (S.C.M. Press, London, 1947).
5 John M. T. Barton, *Penance and Absolution,* pp. 112–15, discusses the decree of the fourth Lateran Council (1215), the comment of the Council of Trent about it, and the precept of the Church about confessing once a year (Faith and Fact Book, Burns, Oates and Washburne, London).
6 I quote Cardinal Newman's passage on confession from *A Newman Anthology,* compiled by William Samuel Lilly, p. 296 (Dennis Dobson, London, 1875). The excerpt is in fact taken by Lilly from Newman's *Present Position of Catholics.*